Henry Richard

Letters and Essays on Wales

Henry Richard

Letters and Essays on Wales

ISBN/EAN: 9783744688994

Printed in Europe, USA, Canada, Australia, Japan

Cover: Foto ©Thomas Meinert / pixelio.de

More available books at **www.hansebooks.com**

LETTERS AND ESSAYS ON WALES.

LETTERS AND ESSAYS

ON

WALES.

BY

HENRY RICHARD, M.P.

London:

JAMES CLARKE & CO., 13 & 14, FLEET STREET.

1884

INTRODUCTION.

I HAVE been urged to reprint some of the papers I have written from time to time on the subject of Wales. It has fallen to my lot to be in some humble measure an interpreter between Wales and England. For though I have lived in London for fifty-three years, I have retained my attachment to, and my interest in, my native land, have kept up my acquaintance with its language and literature, and, through them, with its social, political, and religious condition. At the commencement of the period to which I have referred, little was accurately known in England about the Principality. Railways did not exist. Travelling was difficult, and still comparatively rare; while the difference of language was a formidable impediment to free social intercourse. Hence there arose misconception, prejudice, and, to some extent, mutual repulsion. With all the admirable qualities of the Anglo-Saxon race, an aptitude for understanding, appreciating, and assimilating other races, is not one of its most marked endowments. What tended very much to aggravate the alienation was the known prevalence of Dissent in Wales, which in those days, more perhaps than in these, was regarded in some English circles as almost a crime. And so it came to

A 2

pass that the state of things in Wales was misunderstood, and consequently misrepresented. I did my best to stand in the breach, to defend the character of my countrymen against severe assaults made on their intelligence and morality—the offspring partly of ignorance, and partly of ecclesiastical prejudice—and especially to direct the attention and enlist the interest of English Nonconformists towards their brethren in the Principality. In 1844, I was appointed, in conjunction with the Rev. John Blackburn, to visit the Congregational Churches of Wales, as a deputation from the Congregational Union. On my return, I prepared two reports—one on the religious state of the Principality, which was presented to the Union at its autumnal meeting at Norwich in that year, and which, I think, did something to bring the Nonconformists of England and Wales into nearer relations, and into closer sympathy with each other; the other, on the state of education in Wales, was presented to the Congregational Board of Education. On my suggestion, that body called a Conference on Education at Llandovery, in which they were joined by the Wesleyan Committee on Education. It was a large and representative gathering. A " South Wales Committee on Education " was formed, which led to the institution of a Normal School for Training Teachers, first at Brecon and then at Swansea, and directly or indirectly to the establishment of a large number of day-schools in the various counties of South Wales.

In 1847, I had an opportunity of rendering, if I may presume to say so, another service of some importance to my countrymen. Just before that the Commissioners appointed to inquire into the state of education in Wales had published their report. I dare say they meant to report honestly, but they were singularly disqualified for their work: they had no knowledge of the language, they had no sympathy with the people, and they fell into bad hands. The consequence was a picture of the condition of the country which astounded the whole nation, and certainly no part of it more so than the Principality itself. What the character of that picture was may be learnt from the impression it produced on the English Press. The *Morning Chronicle* of that day declared that "Wales was fast settling down into the most savage barbarism." The *Examiner*, on its authority, stated that the Welsh people "were sunk in the depths of ignorance, and in the slough of sensuality, and that their habits were those of animals, and would not bear description." Other papers expressed themselves in language quite as strong. Stung by a sense of intolerable insult and wrong, a universal cry of indignation arose from every part of Wales. There were, of course, many vehement protests. Mine was made in the form of a lecture delivered at Crosby Hall, in the City of London, to a crowded audience, who for two hours and a-half listened with unflagging interest to my exposure of the gross character of that base libel on the Welsh nation. It was published in a paper called the *British Banner*, which had then a large circulation among Nonconformists, and afterwards in a volume entitled "The Crosby Hall Lectures."

I once thought of reprinting that lecture in this volume; but on reading it I find that the names of many persons are mentioned, some of whom are dead, and others of whom I hope and believe have repented them of the evil they did to my poor countrymen. And so, perhaps, it is better to let it rest. I need not say that this effort was received with exuberant gratitude by my warm-hearted countrymen. The lecture was thought of sufficient importance to call forth a pamphlet in reply from one of the Commissioners in the form of a letter, addressed, if I remember aright, to Lord John Russell.

Later on, in the year 1866, I had an opportunity, through the columns of the *Morning* and *Evening Star*, to publish a series of Letters on the Social and Political Condition of Wales, which are here reprinted. After the election of 1868, when the Welsh people, for the first time, boldly asserted their own independence, the Conservative press in London was made the vehicle for a series of fierce attacks by means of anonymous letters on Welsh Dissent, and especially Welsh Dissenting Ministers. They were charged with being "supporters of anarchy and plunder," with "actively teaching the people to commit arson and murder," and with "scarcely preaching a sermon that was not full of sedition." The editor of the *Daily News* permitted me the use of his columns to repel these false and foul aspersions, and my letter was afterwards published as a small pamphlet with the title of "Calumnies on Welsh Dissent." In 1871 I wrote an article on "The Established Church in Wales," which was subsequently issued as a separate pamphlet, and which is also reproduced here. In 1882, at the invitation of the Committee of the Congregational

Union, I delivered a lecture at the Memorial Hall in Farringdon Street, on "Nonconformity in Wales," which appeared first in the *Nonconformist* newspaper, and afterwards among the "Jubilee Lectures," which have been published in two goodly volumes by the Committee of the Union. I have not thought it necessary to include that in the present volume, as it passes in part over the same ground traversed in the former publications mentioned.

In the year 1882 there appeared an article in the *Church Quarterly Review*, taking as its text the Report of the Departmental Committee on Intermediate and Higher Education in Wales, of which I had the honour to be a member. This production was a vehement attack upon myself for the part I had taken on that Committee, and, through my sides, on Welsh Nonconformity and the people of Wales generally. My friend Dr. Allon offered me the pages of the *British Quarterly Review* for a reply, of which I was glad to avail myself, and my article appeared in that periodical in April, 1883. It was published anonymously; but though it is partly in self defence, I know no good reason why I should now hesitate to avow the authorship.

I have said that I have attempted to act as a sort of interpreter of Wales to England. As a proof that my efforts have not been altogether in vain, I venture to cite the following kind and generous words spoken by Mr. Gladstone at a Welsh National Eisteddfod at Mold, in August, 1873, words which he substantially repeated on another occasion :—" I will frankly own to you that I have shared at a former time, and before I had thus acquainted myself with the subject, the prejudices which prevail to some extent in England and among Englishmen with respect to the Welsh language and antiquity; and I come here to tell you how and why I have changed my opinion. It is only fair that I should say that a countryman of yours, a most excellent Welshman, Mr. Richard, M.P., did a great deal to open my eyes to the true state of the facts by a series of letters which some years ago he addressed to a morning journal, and which he subsequently published in a small volume, that I recommend to the attention of all persons who may be interested in the subject."

I am afraid the reader will find some repetitions in this collection of articles, which it was not very easy to avoid while dealing with substantially the same topics at considerable intervals of time.

22, BOLTON GARDENS,
      December, 1883.

PREFACE TO FIRST EDITION

OF THE

LETTERS ON THE SOCIAL AND POLITICAL CONDITION OF WALES.

THE following letters first appeared in the *Morning* and *Evening Star* from February to May last. It is in compliance with an earnest desire expressed by many who read them in that journal that they are now republished in the present form.

In dealing with such questions as are discussed here, it was not possible to avoid provoking some antagonism. But there has been much less of it than the author had anticipated, while the general interest which these letters have excited in Wales, and the cordial welcome with which they have been greeted by, he may fairly say, the great majority of his countrymen, prove at least the warmth of their hearts and their readiness to recognise and appreciate any honest attempt to serve their interests. The letters have been reproduced *in extenso* in several English papers in Wales, and have been translated for at least three of those published in the Welsh language.

They have been also the subject of approving resolutions in a large number of meetings both in Wales and among the Welsh in England. The author ventures to insert in an appendix some of those passed by important religious associations. He does this, not for the gratification of personal vanity, though it would be mere affectation to deny that it *has* been gratifying to him in a high degree to receive so many spontaneous and generous expressions of approval from such honoured and influential bodies ; but they are inserted here because they ratify, by the testimony of numerous and most competent witnesses, the substantial accuracy of the statements and representations given in the letters.

October, 1866.

LETTERS

ON THE

SOCIAL AND POLITICAL CONDITION OF THE PRINCIPALITY OF WALES.

LETTER I.

PAST RELIGIOUS AND MORAL CONDITION OF WALES.

It is surprising how little accurate knowledge there exists in England as to the state of the Principality of Wales. There are plenty of Englishmen, of course, who are familiar enough with the physical aspects and resources of the country. They know that some parts abound in romantic and picturesque scenery, the delight of tourists and sketchers, and other parts in varied mineral treasures, which pour a rich stream of wealth into the lap of their fortunate possessors. But of the state of society there; of the condition, the character, and feelings of the people, there prevail only the vaguest and cloudiest conceptions. The general impression is that they are a simple, warm-hearted, good-natured race, who talk a strange guttural jargon, and whom John Bull rather likes condescendingly to patronise. But they are deemed greatly behind their Saxon neighbours, very uninstructed, and only half-civilised—for there is a lurking conviction at the bottom of most Englishmen's hearts, that no people can be really civilised who don't talk English. What is known by many beyond this is only mis-known, having been drawn from sources wholly

B

untrustworthy. Some seventeen or eighteen years ago the Government appointed a commission to inquire into the state of education in the Principality of Wales. It consisted of three young barristers, who went about their work in utter ignorance of the language, the character, and all the social and religious peculiarities of the people. While groping about in the dark for some means of acquiring the information they were in search of, they fell into the hands of one class, who hoodwinked and misguided them in every possible way. The result of their labours was presented to the public in the form of three enormous blue-books, containing a picture of the people, as respects their intelligence, morality, and religion, which was unhesitatingly, and with singular unanimity, pronounced by all who had any real acquaintance with the country, to be a gross and hideous caricature. Unhappily, however, coming from men who in some sense represented the Government, it was widely accepted in England as a true representation, and some traditionary echo from those huge official libels still lingers in many minds.

I gladly avail myself, therefore, Mr. Editor, of the opportunity you have kindly offered me to write to you a few letters on the social and political condition of the Principality of Wales. But as the social and political condition of the country is closely connected with its religious condition, it is necessary that I should first call your readers' attention to the latter.

It may be stated in general terms that the Welsh are now a nation of Nonconformists. They became so, in the first instance, not by the force of abstract reasoning against Establishments, or in favour of the principles of Dissent, but simply because they were compelled to look beyond the pale of the Endowed Church for the means of spiritual instruction which were denied them within its pale. I must ask permission to illustrate this point at some length. That is necessary in order to explain much that is peculiar in the present attitude and feelings of the Welsh people. Besides, the story itself is singularly instructive, and serves to throw no little light upon several practical questions that are coming more and more into discussion among ourselves.

For nearly a century after the settlement of the Protestant Reformation in this country, Nonconformity had scarcely any existence in Wales. For a few pious clergymen who, towards the close of that period, were silenced or driven out of their livings for their uncanonical excess of zeal can scarcely be called Nonconformists. Never, therefore, had any Church a fairer opportunity to show what it could do to civilise and Christianise a people than the Established Church had in those days in the Principality. It had the field wholly to itself, and could pursue its labours undistracted by—what it has so often since pleaded in excuse of its want of success—the impertinent intrusion of schismatic interlopers. And how did it employ that golden interval? It is scarcely possible to draw a darker picture than has been drawn by the pens of Churchmen themselves of the state of their Church at that period, and for a long time after. Simony, nepotism, non-residence, pluralism, every form of ecclesiastical abuse, ran riot in the Welsh Church. The great body of the clergy were ignorant, irreligious, immoral, in every way utterly incompetent to fulfil the duties of their office. And, indeed, many of them did not even attempt to fulfil their primary duty as instructors of the people. A chain of testimonies extending over two centuries and a half is at hand to sustain this charge. My space will admit of my citing only a few. In the year 1560 Dr. Meyrick, Bishop of Bangor, states that he had only two preachers in all his diocese. Strype, in his life of Archbishop

Parker, says of the same see in 1565 that there was " no preaching used, and pensionary concubinacy was openly continued, that is allowance of concubines to the clergy by paying a pension, notwithstanding the liberty of marriage granted." In investigating a charge of misgoverning his diocese, brought against Dr. William Hughes, Bishop of Bangor, in 1587, it came out that the bishop himself held sixteen rich livings *in commendam;* that most of the other great livings were in possession of persons who lived out of the country ; and that only three preachers resided on their livings. Nor was this state of things much changed for the better during the next eighty or ninety years. The Rev. John Edwards, one of the clergy ejected by the Parliamentary Commission for Scandalous Ministers, appointed under the Commonwealth, and whose testimony must therefore be held unimpeachable on this point, acknowledges that, at that time, not one in fifteen of his clerical contemporaries could read or write the Welsh language. In 1677 a pious clergyman addressing his brethren says, " There are to be found in each of the Welsh dioceses from forty to sixty churches without a sermon on Sundays," and that at a time, be it remembered, when preaching was the only means of religious instruction that was open to the people.* The biographer of the Rev. Thomas Charles of Bala, a clergyman who became one of the founders of Methodism towards the latter half of the last century, speaking of the condition of North Wales before that excellent man began his apostolic labours, says :—

The Church ministers were in a most degenerate state, both as to principles and practice, while the gentry used no influence in favour of religion or good morals, but themselves gave example of many kinds of wickedness.

---

* For more evidence on the subject relating to this and other periods see " The History of Nonconformity in Wales," by Thomas Rees, D.D., a work of great labour and research, as well as of conscientious accuracy.

Sir Thomas Phillips, in his very able work on Wales, published in 1849, in a chapter designed to show " the various influences by which the Church in Wales has been weakened," draws such a picture, from facts coming down almost to our own day, of lay official delinquency, of episcopal rapacity and nepotism, of misuse of patronage, of clerical incompetence, and, in general, of utter and contemptuous neglect of the moral and spiritual interests of the people, as forms a terrible indictment against the Church, of which he was, nevertheless, the fervid admirer, and into whose bosom he would fain have won back again all his schismatic countrymen. I can only find room for one sentence out of a long passage in which he summarises the contents of that chapter :—

We have found (he says) the ecclesiastical rulers of this clergy and chief pastors of the people, as well as many other holders of valuable Church preferment, to consist often of strangers to the country, ignorant alike of the language and character of the inhabitants, by many of whom they are regarded with distrust and dislike; unable to instruct the flock committed to their charge, or to teach and exhort with wholesome doctrine, or to preach the word, or to withstand and convince gainsayers in the language familiar to the common people of the land.

It is hardly necessary to ask what was the moral and religious condition of a people left to the tender mercies of such a Church. It would be difficult indeed to find language too strong to describe the utter moral desolation into which the whole land had fallen. The Rev. Rees Pritchard, of Llandovery—a name still held in deep veneration throughout the Principality—a pious, eloquent, devoted clergyman, the only one of his class in that age, so far as we know, to whom such a description could apply, who flourished between the years 1602 and 1646, has left a most deplorable picture of the state of the country in his time. He states that not one in a hundred of his countrymen could read ; that no copy of the Scriptures was found even in the mansions of many of

the gentry; that the clergy were asleep, leaving the
people to wallow in their sins, unwarned and unrebuked;
that the upper classes, with rare exceptions, were totally
regardless of religion, and the common people ignorant
and unwilling to receive instruction.

Licentiousness (he says), drunkenness, dishonesty, falsehood,
and infidelity are rampant through the Principality. Judges
and juries sympathise with drunken murderers, and permit
extortioners to rob widows and orphans. Sheriffs and their
deputies plunder innocent people by virtue of their offices. The
Lord's Day is a day for drunkenness, dancing, idleness, games,
and wanton lewdness among the Welsh.

There was considerable improvement during the next
century. But this was owing almost entirely to the
exertions of the Nonconformists, who began at that time
to establish themselves in Wales. Though they were the
victims of incessant annoyance and outrage, not merely
from legal persecutions, but from mob violence, often
instigated by the upper classes, they laboured hard, and
not without effect—principally, however, in South Wales
—in the cause of knowledge, virtue, and religion. But
they were still comparatively few in number and limited
in influence, and the country, as a whole, remained vir-
tually in possession of the Church during the whole of
that period. The change by which the great bulk of the
people passed over to the ranks of Dissent took place at
the rise of Methodism, about the middle of the last century, which gave a wonderful impulse to all bodies of
Nonconformists. But what was the state of the country
before and up to that epoch? It would be easy to multiply testimonies on this point. But let one or two
suffice. Take, first, that of the Rev. Thomas Charles, to
whom I have previously referred, a man who did inestimable service in the cause of education and religion in
Wales. The description, however, must be understood
as applying principally to North Wales. But then that
was precisely the part of the country where the reign of

the Church was all but undisputed. Referring to the middle of the 18th century, Mr. Charles says :—

In those days the land was dark indeed ; hardly any of the lower ranks could read at all. The morals of the country were very corrupt, and in this respect there was no difference between gentle and simple, laymen and clergymen. Gluttony, drunkenness, and licentiousness prevailed throughout the whole country.

And speaking of a still later period, about 1785, he says :—

In my journeys through many parts of North Wales I found that the condition of the people was so low with regard to religious instruction that there was scarcely one in twenty in many places who could read the Bible, and in some places, after special inquiry, it was difficult to find even one who had been taught to read.

Mr. A. J. Johnes, an able and accomplished man, himself a member of the Church of England, in an essay which he published in 1832, " On the Causes of Dissent in Wales," states the following as " the conclusions to which he was irresistibly led " by the whole course of his inquiry—conclusions which very effectually dispose of the complaint sometimes made that the Dissenters have seduced the people from the Church :—

1. That before the rise of Methodism in Wales the churches were as little attended by the great mass of the people as now.

2. That indifference to all religion prevailed as widely then as Dissent in the present day.

It thus apears that the Established Church has, so far as Wales is concerned, utterly failed in her mission. At no period of her history, from the Reformation to this day, has she fulfilled in anything approaching to an efficient and adequate manner her professed function as the instructress of the people. So long as they were left to her care they were abandoned to ignorance, superstition, and gross immorality, while the great bulk of the clergy cared for nothing but the emoluments of their office.

In closing this too long letter, I have only one remark

to add—namely, that all the testimonies I have cited as to the character and influence of the Church in Wales are from Churchmen themselves; I believe there is not a single Dissenter among them.

———

LETTER II.

PERSECUTION OF NONCONFORMISTS AND METHODISTS.

In my former letter I showed, by a series of testimonies taken from Churchmen themselves, how utterly the Church of England had failed in her duty as the moral and spiritual instructor of the Welsh nation. But to say that she failed in her duty is to state only half the truth. She has habitually and strenuously resisted the efforts made by others to supply her own lack of service. The ecclesiastical authorities ever were in the Principality the most active obstructors and persecutors, first of the Puritans, then of the Nonconformists, and finally of the Methodists, in their attempts to diffuse religious know-ledge, and to improve the morals of the people. This is susceptible of proof by a chain of historical evidence coming down from the earliest times to the present.

In the reign of Queen Elizabeth, when, according to the preamble of an Act of Parliament authorising th translation of the Bible into the Welsh language, which however, was not done till thirty years after, " Her Majesty's most loving and obedient subjects, inhabiting within her Highness's dominion and country of Wales, being no small part of this realm, are utterly destitute of God's Holy Word, and do remain in the like, or rather more, darkness and ignorance than they were in the time of Papistry," there arose as an advocate for the Welsh

people a very remarkable man in the person of John
Penry, a native of Breconshire. He was a young clergyman, who had been educated at Oxford, and is described
as having been a "famous preacher in the University."
He was a man of culture and learning, as well as of a
most earnest and heroic spirit. By his writings, and by
his petitions to the Queen and Parliament, he strove hard
to call the attention of the Government and bishops of
that day to the lamentable condition of the Principality.
Nothing can be more powerful and pathetic than his
appeals on behalf of his "dear and native country."
And what was the result? The result was that he was
persecuted and imprisoned for his pains ; and eventually,
after a trial which, as Sir Thomas Phillips truly says,
"disgraces the name of English justice," was hung like
a felon on the prosecution of Archbishop Whitgift.*

When, in the reign of Charles I., some leaven of the
Puritan element, so powerful in England, began to spread
among the clergy in Wales, prompting them to certain
"irregular" efforts for the instruction of the utterly be-
nighted and neglected people, the bishops of the several
Welsh dioceses, at the instigation of Archbishop Laud,
set themselves by a ruthless system of persecution to
root out all such refractory spirits. There is still extant
among the Lambeth MSS. a document which Laud addressed to the King, in which he boasts of the vigorous
proceedings by which the Welsh prelates had driven out
of the Church those who "preached schismatically and
dangerously to the people," and had put down every
species of "Inconformity."† And yet in one part of the
same document the archbishop, while commemorating

* See " Life of John Penry," by Rev. Dr. Waddington.

† "Inconformity" did not mean "Nonconformity," but simply
a refusal to read "The Book of Sports," and other similar obligations, which that imbecile fanatic, Laud, laid on the consciences
of his clergy.

exultingly the complete success with which the Bishop of St. David's had silenced, on the sweeping charge of "Inconformity," some of the zealous men who were really able and anxious to preach, adds with the greatest *naïveté*, "He complains much, and surely with cause enough, that there are few ministers in those poor and remote places that are able to preach and instruct the people." No less significant is the language of mingled triumph and lamentation in which the Bishop of St. Asaph writes to his bigoted primate, that in his diocese "they were not anywhere troubled with Inconformity, but that he heartily wished that they might as well be acquitted of superstition and profaneness."

In like manner the early Nonconformists were incessantly harassed and hunted from place to place "as one doth hunt a partridge on the mountains." "In the times of the Stuarts," says Mr. Johnes in his essay "On the Causes of Dissent in Wales," "dissent from the Episcopal Church became once more an object of persecution; but the ministers of the Welsh Nonconformists still continued to traverse the wild hills of the Principality, braving all dangers for the sake of their few and scattered followers. Their congregations still occasionally met, but it was in fear and trembling, generally at midnight, or in woods and caverns, among the gloomy recesses of the mountains." The Nonconformists in England suffered much in those days. But it may be easily imagined how in a remote district like Wales, at that time far more completely separated from England than at present, the persecutor wantoned in cruel abuse of power.

And, in truth, the imperfect records which still remain prove that the severities practised on the Welsh Nonconformists, if not so sanguinary, were hardly less wearing and grinding than those to which the Covenanters in

Scotland were exposed. Their goods were plundered, their houses were burnt down, their women were grossly insulted, many of the men were beaten within an inch of their lives. The prisons were crowded with them, and that at a time when prisons were hardly fit to be dens for wild beasts. There were several men whose names are still embalmed in the grateful remembrance of their countrymen—Vavasor Powell, Stephen Hughes, &c., who, during this period, laboured most bravely, by preaching and the publication of good books, to supply the spiritual destitution of Wales. But their names are also imperishably associated in the people's hearts with the idea of ecclesiastical and clerical persecution. For just in proportion to the zeal and success with which they toiled for the good of their people was the bitterness of hatred with which they were pursued by those in power. Vavasor Powell was imprisoned no less than thirteen times, and at length died in prison, to which he had been committed by the zeal of a clerical informer. Stephen Hughes, though a man of most inoffensive character as well as of unbounded benevolence, fell under the displeasure, as Dr. Calamy says, of "the conservators of the sacred keys, who passed the censures of the Church upon him, and delivered him to the secular power, who confined him to a close prison in Carmarthen, to the prejudice of his health and hazard of his life." And so with the others.

In the early part of the eighteenth century there arose in the Church in Wales a most excellent man, the Rev. Griffith Jones, of Llanddowror. He did incalculable service to his country by his eloquent preaching, by his various publications in the Welsh language, but especially by the establishment of his remarkable system of Welsh Circulating Schools. Yet though he never left the Church, it is understood that from none of the Welsh bishops, and from very few of the clergy, did he receive the slightest encouragement in his admirable labours. Nay, indeed, he was constantly obstructed and defamed by his clerical brethren, and suffered a persecution for twenty years in the Ecclesiastical Court, because he dared to preach out of his own parish and in unconsecrated places. And it is confidently affirmed that it was a bishop who moved another clergyman to assail him in what is described as " one of the most scurrilous, vulgar, and obscene pamphlets ever issued from the British press."*

So also when the Methodists began their labours, about the middle of the last century, though most of their leaders were at first members, and even ministers, of the Establishment, they were met with the most determined hostility by the clergy. Driven out of the Church to which they were devotedly attached, and in whose service they would gladly have lived and died, had they only been permitted scope for the zeal with which they were consumed on behalf of the multitudes whom they saw sunk in ignorance and irreligion around them, no sooner did they begin to exercise their ministry outside her pale than they were exposed to every species of indignity and annoyance. This was less conspicuously the case in South Wales, because the elder Nonconformists had there to a considerable extent already leavened the mind of the people with religious knowledge, and so prepared them to rally around and protect the zealous clergymen, whose appearance they gladly hailed as a reinforcement of their own ranks. But in North Wales the persecution was terrible, and everywhere the clergy were the leaders. There was a Rev. John Owen in particular, chancellor of Bangor, who dis-

* " A portion of the clergy zealously opposed Mr. Jones, many of the higher classes were systematically opposed to the education of the poor, while the bishops of Wales did not even countenance his measures."—Johnes's Essay.

tinguished himself as a sort of petty Bonner throughout that district. The doings of this man and his associates, as well as the sufferings generally of the early Methodists, have been commemorated in a singularly interesting volume, entitled, "Drych yr Amseroedd" ("The Mirror of the Times"), written some fifty years ago by an old Methodist preacher, partly from his own recollections, and partly from the conversations of older people with whom he had been acquainted. His account has been well summarised by Dr. Rees in the following passage of his history :—

This Owen being a person of considerable talents, a fluent speaker, and a dignitary of the Church, he succeeded in exciting the clergy, and through them the populace throughout the diocese, into a persecuting rage. It was his practice, in which the clergy generally followed his example, to lead a mob to every place where he found that the Nonconformists or Methodists intended to hold a meeting. The inoffensive worshippers were abused, most mercilessly pelted with stones, wounded with knives, shot at; men, and even women, were stripped naked in the presence of the crowd; able-bodied men were pressed for the army or navy, and driven away from their friends and families like cattle, to different parts of England. A full account of the sufferings of the Nonconformists and Methodists in North Wales in the eighteenth century would fill a large volume.*

And, in truth, these persecutions have hardly yet ceased, only that they are now obliged to take another form. It is, if I remember aright, scarcely more than ten years ago since a lady, possessed of a considerable estate in the neighbourhood of Aberystwith, acting notoriously under clerical instigation, served notice upon her tenants, nearly all of whom were Dissenters, that they must either quit their houses and farms or turn Churchmen. And this decree was ruthlessly carried out. Those who refused obedience, though some of them were old people who had occupied their holdings all their lives, and were honoured by the whole neighbourhood for their

* History of Nonconformity in Wales, p. 399.

simple piety and blameless character, were ejected without mercy, while those who succumbed to the menace did so at such a sacrifice of self-respect and reputation as to make them far greater objects of pity than the others who preferred conscience to interest, though they had to suffer so severely for the preference. There are many other humiliations and annoyances to which the Nonconformists of Wales are still frequently exposed, especially as respects sites for their chapels and schools, and the free exercise of the political franchise. To some of these I shall have occasion to advert more at large in my subsequent letters.

I have given this rather lengthened narrative of the past in order to show the reasons why the Welsh have become Dissenters, and why they are likely to continue so. For it is amusing to observe the innocent surprise which some worthy Churchmen still express at their not returning, to use their own favourite phrase, into " the bosom of their spiritual mother." But they forget, or are not aware, that she has never been to them anything but a step mother, who, by her neglect and cruelty drove them to seek a home elsewhere. Nothing can be more explicit on this point than the testimony of the Rev. Griffith Jones, the admirable clergyman to whom I have already referred :—

I must also (he says) do justice to the Dissenters in Wales, and will appeal for the truth of it to all competent witnesses, and to all those themselves who separate from us, that it was not any scruple of conscience about the principles, or orders of the Established Church that gave occasion to scarce one in ten of the Dissenters in this country to separate from us at first, whatever objections they may afterwards imbibe against conforming. No, Sir; they generally dissent at first for no other reason than for want of plain, practical pressing, and zealous preaching, in a language and dialect they are able to understand, and freedom of friendly access to advice about their spiritual state. . . . The people will not believe that there is anything in reason, law, or Gospel that should oblige them to starve their souls to death for the sake of conforming, if their pastor (whose voice, perhaps, they do not know, or who resides a great way from them) will not vouchsafe to deal out unto them the bread of life.*

On the fact alleged in this extract, which is perfectly true, that the Welsh Nonconformists, especially the Methodists, did not in the first instance dissent from "any scruple of conscience about the principles or orders of the Established Church," an attempt was founded some twenty or thirty years ago to coquet a little with, by flattering, the Calvinistic Methodists, a very powerful body in Wales, in hope of luring them back to the fold from which they had wandered. But the promoters of this attempt overlooked the fact that this is the history of nearly all dissent—that the dissidents at first withdraw, not from any objection of principle, but from some abuse or defect in the Church they leave, which has grown intolerable, but that when once outside they become aware of other graver and more radical objections which near proximity, or the blindness of filial affection, had before concealed from their eyes. This has been the process in Wales as elsewhere. The Methodists, who long hankered after the communion they had left, have now become as thoroughly convinced as any class of Dissenters in the Principality, that the grievous evils which their fathers suffered in and out of the Church were not local and temporary accidents, but sprang largely from the very constitution and character of an Establishment. And few things are less likely than that they will ever again seek their religious nourishment from the somewhat withered breasts of their old stepmother.

* Welsh Piety for 1741, pp. 12, 13.

LETTER III.

COMPARATIVE STRENGTH OF THE CHURCH AND NONCON-FORMITY IN WALES.

IN my former letters I have endeavoured to explain the causes which have led to the alienation of the Welsh people from the Established Church, and compelled them to seek refuge in the ranks of Dissent. I will now show the extent to which this has taken place, so as to make good the allegation in my first letter that the Welsh may now, in general terms, be described as a nation of Non-conformists. Our Church friends in the Principality long angrily denied the truth of this allegation, and not without effect in England, though the facts were too noto-rious and patent to every eye in Wales to admit of a moment's doubt. At length came facts from an authori-tative and official source which effectually silenced controversy. Mr. Horace Mann's Report on the Census of Religious Worship, founded on the returns of the Registrar-General for 1851, is so elaborate and exhaus-tive as to leave little to desire down to the period to which it reaches. Some attempts were made by the Bishop of Oxford and others when it was first published to impeach its accuracy. But as those attempts rested upon nothing but *ipse dixit*, and utterly unsupported, assertions, they met with very indifferent success. Their effect, indeed, was rather to confirm and ratify the authenticity of the return. For they led, among other things, to a question being asked of the Government by Mr. Apsley Pellatt, in the House of Commons, to the following effect :—

Whether any recent inquiry had been made into the accuracy of the returns of the Registrar-General, and whether in consequence any doubt existed as to their fairness; also, whether there was any reason for suspecting that the Dissenting returns had been exaggerated, so that the number of attendants at the Established Church on the census Sunday had been made to appear comparatively below the truth.

To which Lord Palmerston, who was then Home Secretary, made the following very explicit reply:—

I have made inquiries on the subject, and I entertain no doubt as to the accuracy of the returns with regard to all the facts to which they refer. Of course, I speak generally, because in returns collected from such a large number of places and furnished by such a variety of persons there may have been inaccuracies one way or the other, which must, to a certain extent, affect those results. My belief is, however, that those inaccuracies could have no sensible effect upon the general results from the facts stated in the returns. I repose sure confidence in the general accuracy of the returns, and in the diligence and care of those under whose arrangements they had been made, by whom I believe every means were taken to render their statements as accurate as possible.

How does the case stand, then, as between the Church and Nonconformity in the Principality as illustrated by these unimpeachable returns? I am indebted for the following analysis to a most able and accurate statistician:—

STATISTICS OF CHURCH AND DISSENT IN WALES (1851).

The population of Wales, including Monmouthshire, in 1851, was 1,118,914. The total number of places of worship was 4,006. —Census, Table B., p. cxciv.:—

PLACES OF WORSHIP.

Of the places of worship—
The Established Church furnished 1,180
Nonconformists. 2,826

Total 4,006

SITTINGS.

Of the sittings (including estimates for defective returns)—
Established Church furnished . 301,897 or 30 per cent.
Nonconformists . . . . . . 692,339 or 70 per cent.

Total 994,236

C

SITTINGS AND POPULATION.

Assuming, as Mr. Horace Mann assumes, that there should be church accommodation for 58 per cent. of the population, or for 689,569 persons in Wales, the above figures show the following results :—

	Sittings.
The Church falls short of this demand by . .	387,672
Nonconformists exceed the demand by . . .	2,770

The Church, that is to say, has provided sittings for only 25 per cent. of the population, while the Nonconformists have provided sittings for nearly 59 per cent. Voluntaryism, therefore, has alone furnished all the accommodation for religious worship that the whole population of Wales requires. The Established Church has not furnished half the accommodation that the people require.

WORSHIPPING POPULATION.

On March 31st, 1851, the worshipping population of Wales was as follows :—*

Church	138,719 or 22 per cent.
Nonconformist	473,102 or 78 per cent.
Total	611,821

These figures are confirmed by the table (N. p. ccc.) of the number of persons present at the most numerously attended services on the Census Sunday. They were—

Churchmen	134,940 or 21 per cent.
Nonconformist	490,543 or 79 per cent.

But, in truth, the above showing very considerably understates the comparative numerical superiority of the Dissenters. At that time, for reasons which I shall hereafter explain, a large number of the children of Dissenters attended Church schools on week days. All of these, together with many of the domestics and dependents of the gentry who were Dissenters, were compelled to attend the Church occasionally. This was particularly the case on the Census Sunday, when, as is well known, special efforts were made to muster a larger attendance

* These figures are obtained on the principle adopted by Mr. Mann, in Table 22 of the Census, and explained by him as follows :—That one-half of those attending in the afternoon, and one-third of those attending in the evening, are new attendants (p. clv.).

than usual. In the opinion of a gentleman than whom few men are better acquainted with Wales, that would have made a difference of nearly 25 per cent. to the Dissenting returns. "The proportion of Dissenters to Churchmen throughout the Principality," says the same authority, "may be put down as one to eight; but in many of the rural and manufacturing districts the preponderance of Dissenters is much greater."

But another accomplished statistician, the late Mr. Plint, of Leeds, has dealt with the returns in a different manner, with a view to show the comparative *progress* of Church and Dissent in the Principality. I must, however, premise, in order to explain any discrepancy that may appear between the two sets of figures, that Mr. Plint does not include Monmouthshire in his analysis, as is done in that which I have just cited. His object is to show the comparative state of the Church and Dissent in 1801 and in 1851.

North Wales, in 1801, stood thus as to religious accommodation :—

	Sittings.	Proportion to all Sittings.
Church of England. . . .	99,216	. . 75·2
All others	32,664	. . 24·8
Total	131,880	. . 100

In the fifty years following the population increased from 252,765 to 412,114, or 63 per cent. To have kept up the ratio of sittings to population by each of these sections of religionists the former should have supplied 62,505 sittings, and it did supply 16,614. The latter ought to have supplied 20,576, and it did supply 217,928. The Church of England fell short of its duty 73·5 per cent., and all other denominations exceeded it 960 per cent. The ratio of sittings to population, which, in 1801 was 52·1 per cent. (5·9 less than the proper standard

C 2

according to Mr. Horace Mann), was in 1851, 88·9—that is, 30 per cent. above it.

South Wales, in 1801, stood thus :—

	Sittings.	Proportion to all Sittings.
Church of England . . .	133,514	. . 61·8
All others	82,443	. . 38·2
Total . . .	215,957	. . 100

The population increased from 288,892 to 593,607, or 105·5 per cent. The quota of sittings required of the Church was 140,854; it did provide 15,204. The other denominations ought to have provided 86,975; they did provide 270,510. The Church of England fell short of its duty 89 per cent.; the other denominations exceeded it 211 per cent. The ratio of sittings to population in 1801 was 74·7 per cent., and in 1851, 84·5. Can the force of antithesis go further ?*

I have not the materials for showing how the proportion stands at the present time. It is well known that at the last census, Churchmen strenuously and successfully resisted the proposal to have the statistics of religious worship taken on the same principle as in 1851. But it may be very confidently affirmed that the proportion of Churchmen and Dissenters has not, in Wales, at least, altered during that interval to the disadvantage of the latter. I find that in the course of the fifteen years that have since elapsed, the Nonconformists have added 281 to the number of their chapels, while many others have been greatly enlarged. I have endeavoured to find the number of churches added, but I regret to say, without success. We may, however, fairly assume from our knowledge of the past that the increase falls very far below that of the chapels as given above.

* 'Voluntaryism in England and Wales; or the Census of 1851 " pp 62-3   London : Simpkin, Marshall and Co.

At the present time (1866) the number of Nonconformist places of worship in Wales, including Monmouthshire, is as follows. The figures in the first three lines are cited from the Year Books of the respective denominations to which they relate, where every chapel is specified by name. For the statistics of the different Wesleyan bodies I am indebted to a very able paper on the state of Wales, published two or three years ago in a volume of " Essays and Lectures" by the Rev. John Thomas of Liverpool :—

Calvinistic Methodists	975
Independents	839
Baptists	589
Wesleyan Methodists (Old Body)	510
Primitive Wesleyan Methodists	100
Minor Wesleyan Bodies	45
Unitarians	30
Society of Friends	7
Roman Catholics	12
Total	3,107

To which must be added that the Welsh have at this time 120 chapels in England, for so great is their attachment to their ancient language, and so deep their solicitude for the religious instruction of themselves and their children, that as soon as any considerable number of them settle in any town or district, their first care is to erect a place for worship and religious instruction in their native tongue.

It would be easy, were it necessary, to add much confirmatory evidence of an incidental kind as to the enormous preponderance of Nonconformists over Churchmen in Wales. The reports presented by the inspectors of schools to the Committee of Council on Education abound with such evidence. Take the testimony of Mr. J. Bowstead, inspector of British Schools, in his report for 1855. After stating that the proportion of Churchmen among the trading and working classes in South Wales certainly does not exceed one to every five, he adds—

Even this proportion, however near the truth, as an average for the whole district, is much too high for many populous localities. I have myself incidentally become acquainted with the result of a minute examination, made in one of the valleys in Monmouthshire, from which it appeared that whilst the Church claimed 20 families within a given area, the Protestant Dissenters claimed 300.*

Still more striking is the testimony of the Rev. H. Longueville Jones, inspector of Church of England schools in Wales. Speaking of the difficulty he had in examining the children in National schools on religious subjects, he says :—

The number of children in Welsh schools, whose parents belong to the Church, is so very small, that it requires great experience and delicacy of feeling to treat their young minds as they should be.†

He gives the statistics of one school in the neighbourhood of Merthyr, which, as it is the only example he cites, he wishes, I presume, to be regarded as an illustration of his meaning. In this school, out of 107 children, only five were of parents belonging to the Church. And when he brings forward the same school in the following year, the table shows the number of children at 144, of whom two only were of Church-going parents. Further to illustrate the progress of Nonconformity in Wales, I subjoin the following short tabular statement, showing the number of congregations at five different periods :—

1742.	1775.	1816.	1861.	1866.
110	171	993	2,927	3,107

Now these facts are of very pregnant significance in their bearing upon one of the most important controversies of our day—namely, the comparative efficiency of an

* Minutes of Council 1855-6, p. 638.
† Minutes of Council 1854-5, p. 602.

endowed and a voluntary Christianity. It cannot be denied that the experiment has been made in Wales under circumstances which give it all the force of an *experimentum crucis*. The people for the most part were poor and scattered. They had to contend with the dead weight, or rather, indeed, with the active and in many instances virulent hostility, of a well-dowered Established Church. From those who might be regarded as their natural leaders, the local gentry, they have had little help and much hindrance. Owing to distance of place and difference of language they were until quite recently shut out to a large extent from the knowledge and sympathy of their wealthier Nonconformist brethren in England and Scotland. And yet in the face of all this behold the result.

The advocates of religious establishments are wont to say that the voluntary principle may work very well under certain favourable circumstances, but that in certain other circumstances it must and will entirely fail. There are two kinds of population especially with whose necessities, they are wont to allege, it is quite unfitted to cope. The first is, that in mining and manufacturing districts, where the rate of increase is so rapid, that it can be overtaken only by the resources and machinery of a State-endowed Church. Well, we have just such a district in that part of the country of which we are now speaking. Monmouthshire and Glamorganshire are the two counties which, of all those in England and Wales, have made the most rapid strides in population since the beginning of the present century. In each of these the number of inhabitants has very much more than tripled within the period named. In the former the increase of population between 1801 and 1851 was at the rate of 244, and in the latter at the rate of 231 per cent., the average rate of increase for the whole of Great Britain in the same time being 93¼ per ·cent. Let us see, then, how the voluntary principle and "the resources and machinery of an Establishment" have respectively coped with this population.

I take from the census of 1851 the registration districts of Merthyr Tydvil, Bridgend, Neath, and Swansea, having an aggregate population of 193,504, in the very thickest part of that mining and manufacturing country ; and I find that the total number of sittings provided by all religious bodies in this district was 68 per cent. on the population, which is 10 per cent. more than the number required according to the calculations of Mr. Horace Mann. But of this number the Church of England provided 14·5, and the Dissenters 53·5 per cent. I take again the districts of Abergavenny and Pontypool, which, I suppose, is the densest part of Monmouthshire, with a population of 87,222. The total number of sittings provided in this district was 75·9 per cent. on the population, of which the Church of England supplied 19·4, and the Dissenters 56·5. Your readers may conceive what would have been the moral and religious condition of the people in those districts if they had been left to "the resources and machinery" of the Establishment.

But there is another kind of population for which, our Church friends declare yet more confidently, the voluntary principle is wholly unadapted—namely, that in rural districts, where the inhabitants are few, scattered, and poor. Nothing, we are assured, but the parochial system, where the State provides a building and a teacher for the people, will meet such a case.

Well, here again Wales supplies us with sample districts of unexceptionable character. I take the registration districts of Cardigan, Newcastle-Emlyn, Lampeter, Aberayron, Aberystwyth, and Tregaron, comprising, I believe, the whole of my native county of Cardiganshire, with an aggregate population of 97,614. In this district the number of sittings provided was 97·8 per cent. on the population, of which the Church of England supplied 27·4, and the Dissenters 70·4 per cent.

I will take another part of the country, which may be regarded as of a somewhat mixed character—namely, Carnarvonshire; for though it is mainly agricultural, there is among the large slate-quarries a considerable population that may be called mining and manufacturing. And how do matters stand there? Why, thus :—Taking the registration districts of Pwllheli, Carnarvon, Bangor, and Conway, with a population of 94,674, the total number of sittings provided was 95·1 per cent. on the population, of which the Church of England supplied 28·2, and the Dissenters 66·9 per cent.

From these facts there are some inferences that are obvious and irresistible. They prove—First, that the Church of England is not the Church of Wales; secondly, that, but for the exertions of the Nonconformists, Wales would have been at this time, as regards its spiritual interests, in a most pitiable plight. A most estimable clergyman, a native of Wales, whose name is still venerated by many in this metropolis, the Rev. William Howels, of Long Acre, once said that, but for the Methodists and Dissenters, the devil might long ere this have claimed the Principality as his own special diocese. Thirdly, that the voluntary principle, when fairly worked, is sufficient to supply the spiritual wants of a nation, seeing that the Welsh, amid poverty, isolation, and discouragement, have provided themselves with more ample means of religious worship and instruction than can be found, perhaps, among any people under the face of heaven.

LETTER IV.

AGENCIES IN THE EVANGELISATION OF WALES.

In my last letter I showed the rapidity and completeness with which the inhabitants of Wales have provided themselves with the means of religious worship and instruction. And surely the phenomenon is sufficiently noteworthy to deserve being examined a little, which thus shows a poor and secluded people, after having been so long neglected by those who had professedly taken charge of their spiritual interests, suddenly quickened into a new life, rising to the work of providing for their own wants, and from very scanty resources, in less than a century, covering the whole face of the country with an array of 3,000 places of worship, where they sustain a religious apparatus as extensive, and, for its purposes, I venture to say, as effective as can be found in any part of the kingdom, or, perhaps, of the world. I hope to make it clear in my future letters, from facts which none can dispute, that this has been attended with the most beneficent influence on the character of the entire nation, changing a people who were before deplorably ignorant, superstitious, and depraved, into a community in a high degree enlightened, moral, and pious. It may be worth while, therefore, to inquire a little into the means by which this transformation has been effected; and as the inquiry will help to throw great light upon some of the most characteristic qualities and habits of the people, it cannot but be regarded as germane to the object of these letters.

There were three things, I conceive, which mainly contributed to the remarkable results which I have indicated. First, the surpassing power of the Welsh pulpit; secondly, the influence of the " Private Society," as it is called, a peculiar institution, the offspring of Methodism, which I shall endeavour to explain; thirdly, the system of Sunday-schools, which is also of a peculiar character, differing widely in many respects from that which prevails in establishments of the same name in England.

From the rise of Methodism at the latter end of the last century, Wales has been supplied with a succession of preachers of rare qualifications for the work given them to do. The first generation of these had passed away before my time. But it was my happiness to be brought up in intimate acquaintance with some of their successors of the next generation. My judgment may, no doubt, be coloured by national partiality. Nor am I unmindful of the delusive halo which imagination throws around the scenes and memories of early life,

> Clothing the palpable and the familiar
> With golden exhalations of the dawn.

But after making large allowance for all this, I think I cannot be mistaken in saying that the great Welsh preachers whom I was constantly hearing in my boy-hood—and the race is by no means extinct yet—were unrivalled masters of sacred eloquence. I have listened to most of the popular preachers that have adorned the English and Scotch pulpits within the last thirty years, and, while cordially acknowledging the eminent merits of some of them, I must still say that none of them have appeared to me even to approach the men I refer to, in their power to move and thrill and subdue a mixed popular audience. They had in an eminent degree that first requisite of all great oratorical success, especially in the pulpit—intense earnestness. Their life was so laborious, self-denying, and devoted, that not a moment's doubt could rest on the minds of their hearers of the lofty impulse by which they were moved, and the perfect simplicity of purpose with which they were seeking, not theirs, but them. But they had, moreover, rare natural advantages for their office. Many of them were men of stately and commanding personal presence, and were endowed with voices of great compass and melody, which by constant use they had learnt so to rule as to express, with the nicest modulation, all the varying moods of an orator's mind. No greater mistake could be committed than to imagine that their preaching consisted of mere loud and incoherent rant, such as is sometimes associated with the idea of Methodist preaching in England. Their sermons were carefully prepared, and often, by frequent repetition, elaborated to a high degree of oratorical perfection, while in their mode of delivery they were distinguished by nothing so much as their absolute self-ossession, the mastery they retained over themselves in the very torrent, tempest, and (as I may say) whirlwind of their passion." It is true that they claimed and exercised unbounded liberty in their methods of exhibiting the truth they believed. They were not restrained by that mortal fear of transgressing "the decencies" which fetters an English preacher, and renders it all but impossible for him to be oratorically effective. They abandoned themselves freely to the swaying impulses of their own inspiration. They used without hesitation or stint all forms of speech that were at their command—trope, metaphor, allegory, graphic pictorial description, bold prosopopœia, solemn invocation, impassioned appeal, dramatic dialogue and action. They did this, not of set purpose, for they might not even know the names that rhetoricians had given to those figures of speech, but because—following the dictates of their own natural genius for oratory—such were the means that seemed best adapted to produce the impression they desired.

The outward accessories, also, which often surrounded them, no doubt contributed largely to the effect of their eloquence. First from necessity, and afterwards from habit, religious meetings were and are in Wales frequently held in the open air. On such occasions the whole population of a district for many miles round, suspending all business and labour, will flock together bodily. I have a vivid remembrance of many of these remarkable gatherings. Sometimes the platform was pitched not far from the sea-shore, the softened murmur of the ocean mingling with, as if it bore burden to, the sound of sacred song that from the assembled multitude

> Rose like a stream of rich-distilled perfume
> And stole upon the air.

Sometimes it was in an open glade, amid rich woodland scenery, a spot being usually chosen where the greensward sloped up gradually from the stage on which the ministers stood, forming a sort of ascending natural gallery, and as the surrounding trees, gently swayed by the wind, bent and rustled, it might almost seem, amid the solemn associations' of the scene, to the excited feelings of the people,

> As if the forest leaves were stirred with prayer.

A preacher of known eloquence standing up on those occasions, when "all impulses of soul and sense" combined to render every heart accessible to impression, found his work already half-done to his hands. He saw a dense mass of human beings in serried array before him, each upturned countenance flushed with that eager and friendly expectation so favourable to a speaker. As he proceeded with his discourse a deep hum of approval —probably inherited from Puritanic times—indicated to him the quick appreciation of his hearers for any skill in argument or felicity of illustration which he might display.

But when the preacher became more animated, his delivery would often pass into a kind of wild recitative, which had an inexpressible charm to the ear, while at the same time it was so free and elastic as to adapt its musical undulations to all forms of solemn warning, awful denunciation, or pathetic appeal, which an impassioned oratory requires. As the excitement gathered and grew the effect was indescribable. Wave after wave of emotion would pass over and thrill through the vast congregation, until it was seen to move and sway to and fro, "as the trees of the wood are moved with the wind." Of the thousands of eyes riveted upon him, the preacher would now see many swimming in tears, while loud sobs and passionate responses from hundreds of voices echoed back his appeals. This again would react upon himself, rousing him to yet greater fervour of eloquence. For, as it has been well remarked, "the man accustomed to these expressions, and habitually looking for them among the 'outward and visible signs' of the effect of his preaching, and who could not preach under their influence with incalculably augmented power, must have been utterly destitute of the oratorical temperament, and never could have been intended by Nature to sway a promiscuous assembly."* It was such preaching as this that roused Wales from its spiritual torpor, and was partly the cause and partly the effect of those remarkable periodical visitations known as religious revivals, a species

* For a fuller description of the characteristics of Welsh preaching, I may refer the reader to a very able essay on the subject by the Rev. J. Kilsby Jones, appended to the "Life of the Rev. William Williams," and to the "Memoir of Christmas Evans," by the Rev. D. M. Evans, a volume of singular interest and beauty.

of phenomena which it is much more easy to sneer at than to explain or wisely appreciate. With some serious drawbacks, no one acquainted with the inner life of the country can doubt that they have been of incalculable value to Wales.

Connected with these, and intended to give form and permanence to the effect they produced, were the " Private Societies" of which I have previously spoken. Like most other institutions that are really useful and well adapted for their purpose, they were neither formally established nor imported, but grew naturally out of the circumstances in which the ministers and the people found themselves. One can readily understand how much bewildered, ignorant, and superstitious minds would feel at the sudden rush upon them of such new thoughts and emotions as would accompany their first vivid apprehension of religious truth. If not wisely handled such a state of mind was quite capable either of subsiding into deeper hardihood of impiety than before, or of passing into the excesses of a wild and dangerous fanaticism. To meet this emergency the founders of Methodism—and this practice has been borrowed from them by every other denomination in Wales, not except-ing the Church of England—were wont to gather their converts into societies, or classes, in order to instruct them more perfectly in the principles of Christianity. Fully aware of the crude condition in which many of their disciples were at the time, the old preachers laid great stress upon this process of " indoctrinating," as they called it, or " egwyddori" as the expressive and untranslatable Welsh word has it. But they did more than this, and that, perhaps, constituted the most power-ful attraction of the private societies. They encouraged the members to speak in presence of the sympathising brotherhood, and, in such stammering accents as they could command, of their own experience of the newly-awakened spiritual life within them, the doubts which assailed them, the hopes which cheered them—the alternations of joy and sorrow, of temptation and triumph, through which they passed. It must be remembered that those who were at the head of the religious movement of which I am now speaking in Wales, were not ignorant men. The first of them were dissident clergymen, the very pick for genius and piety of the ministers of the Establishment. And those who followed them were persons not only of uncommonly vigorous natural faculties, but of very considerable cultivation. Among them were some eminently skilled in spiritual diagnosis, who knew how to guide their neophites with infinite tenderness and skill through the dangers of their early religious career.

No doubt the institutions I have been describing were adapted only for a very primitive state of society, and an uneducated and unsophisticated people. Persons of culture and refinement acquire more reticence on such matters, and shrink from disclosing to the general gaze their innermost and most sacred feelings. There may have been, also, something of national idiosyncrasy in the success of these societies in Wales. The Anglo-Saxon, less imaginative and emotional, and more self-contained and self-sufficing, seems able to dispense with those outward auxiliaries which the impulsive Celtic nature requires. Among the reasons assigned by the Rev. Griffith Jones, the excellent clergyman whose words I quoted in a former letter, for the spread of Dissent in Wales, this was one—that the people when they became religiously impressed, found in the Church "none to unbosom their grief to, none that would patiently hear their complaints and deal tenderly by their souls and dress their wounds; they, therefore, fled to other people for relief, as dispossessed demoniacs will no longer frequent the tombs of the dead." Be that as it may, it cannot be doubted that these institutions were admirably adapted to the condition of the people in the Principality at this time, adding to their faith virtue, and to virtue knowledge ; giving the fixedness of conviction and habit to what was often at first mere emotion, and saving them in a remarkable degree from the mischiefs which sometimes attend uncontrolled religious excitement. But like many other things, the day of their usefulness is obviously past.*

To the influences I have already specified must be added that of the Sunday-schools. These, like many other good things in Wales, owe their origin to the Rev. Thomas Charles, of Bala. There were, however, two men—the Rev. Owen Jones, in North Wales, and the Rev. Ebenezer Richard, in South Wales—a name very dear to the writer of these letters—who gave themselves with indefatigable zeal and labour to the development and organisation of the system which Mr. Charles had began. And now they have become spread over the whole face of the country, so as to cover it like a web.

One peculiarity of the Sunday-schools in Wales is this, that they comprise not the children of the country merely, but a large proportion of the adults. It is a matter of constant lamentation among the promoters of Sunday-schools in England that the elder scholars, when they have acquired a tolerable proficiency in reading, leave the school, and are withdrawn from the salutary influence which might be otherwise exercised

* When I speak of their "usefulness" as "past," I refer to the old method of conducting them, rather than to the institutions themselves. The "societies," wisely adapted to modern requirements, still are, and long may be, eminently useful.

D

over them by their teachers at the most critical period of
their life. But in Wales, however perfectly the young
people may learn to read, they do not dream of quitting
the school. On the contrary, when that acquisition is
made, they frequent it with far more interest than before,
for they then form themselves into classes, under the
guidance of older and more experienced men, for *studying*
the Bible, bringing into the common stock whatever
means of illustration they can command to throw light
over the history, geography, antiquities, and doctrines of
the Book. By this means the people almost universally, not only learn to read with an understanding
mind, but acquire very considerable stores of sound
Scriptural and theological knowledge, which, among
other things, prepare and qualify them to be intelligent and appreciative hearers of their ministers' public
teaching.

Another marked feature of the Welsh Sunday-schools
is the extent to which they employ catechetical instruction. By this, however, we must not understand the
mere learning and perpetual repetition of any one form of
catechism, than which few things are more adapted to
deaden the mind. Far from it. The catechisms in
Wales are innumerable, though in truth the word " catechism " is by no means an adequate equivalent for the
Welsh " Pwnc." The method adopted is this. Some
particular topic is selected for instruction or impression.
At one time it may be some piece of Scripture, history,
or biography ; at another, a leading Christian doctrine ;
at a third, some important moral duty. Let us take as
an example " The Duty of Truthfulness." All arguments
and considerations tending to show the value and sacredness of truth, and the folly and wickedness of falsehood,
are put into the form of questions and answers, which
are sustained by Scripture authority and illustrated by

Scripture example. This is learnt by the entire school and recited sometimes in the presence of the whole congrega· tion. But when the catechist examines them publicly, he by no means confines himself to the questions written before him, for which the answers are prepared. He asks many other extempore questions bearing on the topic in hand, which are intended either to test the Scripture knowledge of the catechumens, or to impress more deeply upon their mind the truths to which the catechism relates. Sometimes the schools of a district, to the number of six or eight, will meet in one place to recite their catechisms, when there is a good deal of emulation as to which shall acquit themselves best, especially in giving quick and satisfactory answers to the extempore questions that may be asked by the ministerial catechists. All this has a marvellous tendency to keep the minds of the people alive, and to enlarge their knowledge in at least one department —that of Scripture and theology, in respect to which kind of knowledge I doubt whether they are surpassed by any nation in the world.

LETTER V. .

THE INTELLECTUAL CONDITION OF WALES.

WHILE, in my former letters, I have been portraying the rapid progress which the people of Wales have made in providing for themselves the means of religious worship and instruction by the multiplication of chapels, Sunday-schools, etc., I have anticipated that such questions as the following would arise in the minds of many of my readers :—Well, and what is the practical result ? What effect has all this produced on the character of the people

D 2

as respects their intelligence and morality? These are questions which I shall endeavour to answer in this and one or two subsequent letters. And it is the more necessary to do this as an attempt has been made to discredit the cause of Nonconformity by blackening the character of the Welsh.

When the Commissioners on Education went down to Wales eighteen years ago (now thirty-five years ago), some of the local clergy—only a small number, I am happy to say—unable to disguise from their visitors the fact that the great bulk of the inhabitants had forsaken their ministrations, tried to find some consolation for their self-love by slandering their neighbours. They first represented the people as grossly ignorant, depraved, and brutal, in order that they might then have the satisfaction of ascribing this their evil case, as some of them did *totidem verbis*, to "the immoral teaching of Dissent." It may be readily imagined that this did not much mend the chances of the reverend gentlemen to recover their lost influence over their countrymen. But such a representation was grossly at variance with fact. There is in Wales, as everywhere else, plenty of evil to be deplored and remedied. But, taken as a whole, and comparing class with class, I doubt whether there is a population on the face of the earth more enlightened and moral, more loyal to the Throne, more obedient to the laws, more exemplary in all the relations of life, than the inhabitants of Wales. These assertions I will try to make good to the satisfaction of your readers.

And first let me say a few words as to the state of education and intelligence among them. I believe that at no period in their history had the people of Wales sunk into that utter mental torpidity which marks—if I may say so without offence—some portions of the English peasantry. Grossly ignorant and superstitious multitudes of them undoubtedly were, through the long ages of neglect of which I have already spoken. But there were always influences at work which saved them from absolute stagnation of intellect. The traditions of their national history—not less fascinating because surrounded with a nimbus of poetic myth—telling of their ancient kings, druids, and bards, of Arthur and Merlin, of Llywarch Hen and Taliesin, of Howell the Good, and Llewelyn " ein llyw olaf " (our last prince), as he is still fondly called—were cherished with great tenacity by the popular mind. A passionate, and, I fear I must add, a fierce and vindictive patriotism, as the patriotism of the past was wont to be, was constantly fed by stories, half fact and half fable, transmitted from father to son, of the cruelty and perfidy of their Saxon and Norman oppressors, and of the victories and defeats which had marked their long struggle for independence, while fighting under the banner of the Red Dragon—stories of the slaughter of the learned monks of Bangor ; of the Alleluia victory ; of " Brâd y Cyllill Hirion ; "* of the massacre of the bards, and others of similar import, which—or at least the evil feelings accompanying them—have happily faded, or are fast fading out of the popular mind. Fragments of poetry and music, coming down from immemorial times, were always floating plentifully in the air. The very superstitions, some fantastic and some terrible, with which the country abounded, acted as a powerful

---

* "The Treason of the Long Knives," a story of the remote past widely current in Wales in my boyhood, and probably so still. It told how the Saxon invaders, unable to defeat the Britons in fair fight, under the guise of friendship invited all the Welsh princes to a great banquet, and, as a further mark of fraternity, proposed that the Britons and Saxons should sit at table alternately ; but, at a signal from their chief, each treacherous Saxon drew his long knife and plunged it into the heart of his neighbour. I am not antiquarian enough to say whether this story is purely legendary, or has any foundation in fact.

stimulant, at least, to the imagination—the belief in magic and witchcraft—the vision of the "Tylwyth Teg," or the "Beautiful Family," as the fairies were called, who

Met on hill, in dale, forest or mead,
By pavèd fountain or by rushy brook,
Or on the bleached margent of the sea,
To dance their ringlets to the whistling wind;

—the "Corpse Bird," which came at night flapping its ominous wings against the windows of the sick man's chamber; the "Corpse Candle," a small blue light seen near a house where a death was soon to take place, and going thence straight to the churchyard; the "teulu," a spectral funeral procession, marching in ghastly silence all over the road along which the doomed person, whose decease it foreshadowed, would soon be carried to his grave. In the worst times, also, the popular merry-makings were never without some intellectual element which saved them from degenerating into mere sensual orgies; for the harp was there, and "pennillion" singing an improvisation in verse accompanying the harp, and in some parts of the country, a sort of broad farces, or dramatic pasquinades, under the name of "interludes," acted by the peasantry. And there were better things than these; for sometimes the people's natural genius for minstrelsy and song would seem suddenly to blossom with even an exuberant fertility. If any one doubts this, he has but to consult the collection of old melodies, and the words to which they were sung, taken down from the lips of the peasants in the vales of Neath and Glamorgan by Miss Jane Williams of Aberpergwm, herself—according to the testimony of Mr. Chorley—"the most exquisite amateur singer he had ever heard." My friend, Dr. Davis, of Swansea, and there are few more competent judges, says of these compositions, "I consider them without exception the finest pastorals I know, and

may be backed against the world for poetry, music, and
purity of sentiment." And those published by Miss
Williams are only a small selection from hundreds which
she noted down from the singing of the country people,
all of which are supposed to have sprung into existence
from about 1680 to 1780.

But while all these things contributed to stir and agi-
tate the popular mind, and save it from subsiding into
that brutish stolidity which is the most fatal of all conditions, the real awakening of the soul of the nation must
be traced to the great religious revival under the Methodists about the middle of the 18th century, for which,
however, there had been long and patient preparation,
not always sufficiently acknowledged, in the quiet
labours, for a century and a half before, of other bodies
of Nonconformists. Still, that, certainly, was the movement which to the country at large was as life from the
dead, and lifted the great mass of the people for the first
time into the enjoyment of something like a moral and
spiritual education; and from that time light and knowledge have gone on steadily diffusing themselves in an
ever-widening circle. Mr. Johnes, in his essay on "The
Causes of Dissent in Wales," alluding to certain explana-
tions of the phenomenon with which some of his brother
Churchmen attempted to comfort themselves, candidly
remarks, " Nothing can be more unsatisfactory than to
rank ignorance and individual eccentricity as in themselves causes of Dissent in Wales; " for the fact is, he
adds, that " Dissent has increased with knowledge, and
not with ignorance."

And what, then, is the present condition of Wales as
respects the intelligence and mental activity of its people?
I know of no better test of this in reference to any people
than the quantity of literature they consume. The oddest
misconceptions prevail in England as to the state of the

Principality in this matter.   I have met with people who
imagined that the Welsh language is only a sort of provincial dialect of English, like that which prevails in
Scotland.   Others think that, though it be, indeed, a
separate language, it is one of the rudest and most elementary description, with little or no regular grammatical
construction, living only as oral speech on the lips of the
most ignorant of the people, and rapidly disappearing
from the face of the earth.   As to the large stores of
ancient literature existing in the Welsh language, I may
refer your readers to an article in a recent number of
the *Cornhill Magazine*, from the pen of Mr. Matthew
Arnold, who, in a slightly patronising, but not ungenerous
spirit, while recommending the Welsh quite coolly to give
up their language, does justice to the extent and value of
the old literary treasures it contains.   But very few
Englishmen seem to know that the Welsh have a large
living literature, and that at no time has the Welsh press
been so active as it is at this moment.

And, first, as to its periodical literature.   I have a
list before me, as accurate as I could make, though I
am afraid not quite complete, of the periodicals issued
in the Welsh language.   Among them I find 5 quarterlies, 25 monthlies, 8 weeklies.   All these have an
aggregate circulation of not less than 120,000 copies.   I
next come to translations from the English language.
Among commentators on the Bible, the following have
been translated into Welsh :—Matthew Henry, Thomas
Scott, Dr. Gill, Dr. Coke, Guise, Burkitt, Brown (of
Haddington), Campbell, Barnes, and Kitto.   Among
English and other authors, some of whose works are
found in Welsh, may be mentioned Calvin, Grotius
Baxter, Owen, Howe, Charnock, Goodwin, Bishop Hall,
Fisher, Brooks, Bunyan, Gurnal, Boston, Watson, Flavel,
Fleetwood, Poole, Colquhoun, Samuel Clarke, Mason,

Harvey, Doddridge, Watts, Jonathan Edwards, Cole, Fawcett, Maclean, Keach, Burder ("Eastern Customs,"), Wesley, Robert Hall, Dr. Chalmers, Abbot, Finney, Angel James, Wardlaw, Gurney, Jenkyn, Dr. King, Dr. M'Cosh, Baptist Noel, Dr. Angus, Walker, Hodge, together with many of the works of the Christian Knowledge Society, and the Religious Tract Society. It will be seen that these are all, or nearly all, religious and theological writers, and the prevailing tendency of the national mind is unquestionably towards that species of literature ; not, however, exclusively. There are at least two translations of " Paradise Lost," and portions of the works of Gray, Young, Cowper, Blair, and other English poets, have been rendered into Welsh, and recently one of the plays of Shakspeare—" Hamlet," I believe. So have Bacon's essays, some of the late Dr. Dick of Scotland's works on science, all Josephus's writings, and at the present time a costly edition of Goldsmith's "Animated Nature" is coming out in parts, with a large circulation. Of original works in the Welsh language it would be vain here to attempt any enumeration. I will only advert to a few serials that are now in course of publication. First, there is a cyclopædia, which will extend to many large volumes, dealing, like other cyclopædias, with the whole circle of human knowledge ; and it appears to me, from the specimens I have seen, to be conducted and written with very great ability. There is a Dictionary of the Bible, to be completed in three large royal octavo volumes. There are two biographical dictionaries now appearing simultaneously. There is a geographical dictionary, illustrated by many excellent maps. There is a work on music, of which twenty-seven shilling parts have already appeared. But the taste of the people runs principally, as already intimated, on Biblical and theological subjects. Perhaps no nation in the world has been so amply supplied with copies of the Scriptures. The Bible Society alone, since its establishment in 1804, has circulated upwards of a million copies in the Principality ; and the demand is still unabated, for last year (1865) nearly 70,000 copies were taken in Wales and Monmouthshire. Of commentaries and other works illustrating the Bible the number and variety is surprising—some of them very elaborate and costly, and all, without exception, securing a large circulation. And there is a lingering prejudice still in many minds, in spite of modern illumination, that there may be worse things for a people than to be thoroughly saturated with the history, poetry, and morality of the Bible. It is rather a striking illustration of the demand for Welsh literature that several enterprising English or Scotch publishing firms, such as Mackenzie and Fullerton, have found it worth their while to issue books in the Welsh language from their presses, and some of them of a very expensive nature.

Your readers must not, however, imagine that the Welsh language is destitute of books on other than Biblical and theological subjects. For works of poetry and music there is an insatiable demand. One publication on congregational psalmody has had a circulation of more than 20,000 copies. In one bookseller's list before me I find no fewer than fourteen works on music published within a few years. There are works also on grammar, arithmetic, geography, chronology, botany, logic, rhetoric, natural philosophy, etc. ; and a series of essays by the Rev. Dr. Edwards, of Bala, in which various literary questions are discussed in a broad spirit, and with eminent ability, is now being issued from Mr. Hughes's press at Wrexham. The Welsh are further pretty well furnished with histories, for among the works on this subject I find a history of the world, a history of

Great Britain, a history of Wales, a history of religion in Wales, a history of the Christian Church, a history of the Calvinistic Methodists, a history of the Independents, a history of the Baptists, etc. And of biographies of their own worthies they have great abundance. "The only books," says one of the principal publishers in Wales, in a letter to me, "that absolutely fail in Welsh are novels."

Now, to estimate rightly the significance of these facts we must bear in remembrance the number and character of the population for which this supply is provided. At the last census the population of Wales, including Monmouthshire, was 1,286,495. Sir Thomas Phillips, and others who have studied the question, divide this into three parts as respects language. One-third are Englishmen who have settled in Wales, or Welshmen who have become Anglicized, and speak the English language only. Another third are competently acquainted with both languages; while the last third use the Welsh language exclusively, and know very little English or none. The whole, therefore, of that body of literature which I have described must be consumed by the two-thirds that know Welsh—or about 850,000 people. But from this must be deducted a very considerable portion of the second class, who, though they may be well acquainted with Welsh, prefer, and pretty much confine themselves to, English literature. Indeed, it may be confidently affirmed that by far the greater part of the issues from the Welsh press are taken by the working classes—miners, workers in slate-quarries, artisans, small farmers, and agricultural labourers.

After the facts I have stated, I think I may fairly ask whether there is any population of the same class in the kingdom among whom the taste for solid reading, and the intelligence and mental activity it indicates, are more conspicuous? But it would be a great mistake to imagine that it is Welsh only that is read in the Principality. There are upwards of thirty English newspapers published in Wales, some of them conducted with great ability and having a large circulation. Of the quantity of English literature circulated in Wales I have failed to procure any very definite statistics. I have only received as the result of my enquiries the impression that it must be very considerable, and is rapidly increasing. One Welsh publisher (Mr. Evans, of Holywell), to whom I wrote on the subject, says : "I can only say in regard to this little town, of about 6,000 inhabitants, that I, who am only one of five booksellers in the town, sell of English papers and periodicals, 90 dailies, 520 weeklies, serials, and periodicals, and 150 monthlies.

LETTER VI.

INFLUENCE OF THE EISTEDDFODAU AND SIMILAR INSTITUTIONS IN WALES.

IN my last letter I endeavoured to illustrate the amount of intelligence and mental activity which prevail among the people of Wales, by giving some idea of the nature and extent of the literature that circulates among them. To those of your readers who did me the honour to examine my statements, it would be apparent, from the predominantly Biblical and theological character of the books which find most acceptance in the country, that the main element in Welsh civilisation is a religious element. There is, however, one other source whence the national mind has received a powerful impulse. I allude to that class of institutions for the cultivation of literature, eloquence, poetry, and music, which are now spread over the whole face of the Principality, and of which the national Eisteddfod is the most conspicuous representative. The meetings of the Eisteddfod have of late years attracted considerable attention in England. But, for some reason or other, the English Press has generally thought fit to take them in high dudgeon. It might have been thought that the spectacle of the remnant of an ancient race, "the great Celtic race which," as Professor Goldwin Smith says, "once covered all Britain as well as Gaul, and probably Spain, and whose sword, at one moment cast into the scale of fate, nearly outweighed the destiny of Rome"—after having for so many centuries bravely guarded their language and national traditions among the mountain fastnesses to which they had been driven by the foot of the invader, meeting, in these modern times, not for any purpose of violence or sedition, but to promote the study of literature and the arts, to preserve from extinction the stores of poetry and music which they had derived from ancestral times, and to diffuse among their people generally a love for such pursuits, would have inspired some feelings of interest and respect in the bosom of every man of liberal taste and generous sympathies. And, in truth, such is the feeling that it has and does inspire among those whom a large and scholarly culture has lifted out of what has been well called the provincial habit of mind—men like Robert Southey, Augustin Thierry, the Chevalier Bunsen, the Bishop of St. David's, and Mr. Matthew Arnold, from whose recent article in the *Cornhill Magazine* I must allow myself the gratification of citing one sentence. "An Eisteddfod is, no doubt," he says, "a kind of Olympic meeting; and that the common people of Wales should care for such a thing shows something Greek in them, something spiritual, something humane, something (I am afraid one must add) which in the English common people is not to be found."

But writers of the "own correspondent" class find nothing in these assemblages but materials for disdain and derision. And although, no doubt, some of the old bardic forms and symbols may be regarded, amid modern surroundings, as being rather practical anachronisms which had better be omitted, it is difficult to read the flippancies with which even these are assailed without applying to the writers the rebuke, slightly altered, which Gower addressed to ancient Pistol for flouting another old Welsh custom, " Will you mock at an ancient tradition begun upon an honourable respect, and worn as a memorable trophy of pre-deceased genius?" Indeed, I cannot account for the extreme bitterness of contempt in which some of the English papers have indulged respecting these, to say the least, very harmless demonstrations, unless it be on the assumption that, taking too much *au pied de la lettre* certain over-fervid oratorical effusions, they imagine that in the assertion of Welsh nationality, customary, and surely not very unnatural or unpardonable on such occasions, there is some lurking disaffection to Saxon rule. And few things are more amusing than the charming unconsciousness with which John Bull betrays his inconsistencies on this matter. For while his sympathy for nationalities oppressed, or compressed, or suppressed by any foreign Power, effervesces so fiercely, that his rulers can with difficulty restrain him from flying at the throat of the greatest military monarchies of Europe in the excess of his zeal on their behalf, yet when any one of the nationalities he has suppressed—and nobody on earth has suppressed so many—dares to " peep, or mutter, or move the wing,"

were it only in so purely sentimental and innocent a way
as is done at a Welsh Eisteddfod, John's jealousy is
aroused, and he becomes straightway as stern, merciless,
inexorable as the Czar Nicholas, when warning the
Polish nobles at Warsaw not to cherish vain illusions.
All I can say is, if such a suspicion ever does cross the
minds of the writers in question, in connection with
Wales, that a more groundless and absurd fantasy never
troubled any man's brain.   I venture to assert that there
is not in the whole extent of the British dominions, from
the Hebrides to the Punjaub, a community more loyal to
the throne of Queen Victoria than the inhabitants of
Wales.

The fact is that the English papers do not understand,
and do not care to take much trouble to try to understand, the significance of the Eisteddfodau.   Their object
is not to foment the feeling of nationality in the political
sense at all.   Nor is it to perpetuate the existence of the
Welsh language, for if its existence depended upon these
meetings its fate would soon be sealed.   The best security
for the duration of the Welsh language is the passionate
attachment of the people to it as the vehicle of religious
worship and instruction.

The true reason why the Eisteddfodau are held is to be
found, partly in the reverence which the common people
of Wales cherish for old customs, and partly in the
genuine delight they take in such intellectual excitements as are afforded them there, in exercises of oratory,
and competitions in poetry and music, just as the common
people of England take delight in horse-racing and fox-
hunting and pugilism. " It is a most remarkable feature,"
said the late Bishop of St. David's, Dr. Thirwall, " in the
history of any people, and such as could be said of no other
than the Welsh, that they have centred their national
recreation in literature and musical competitions."

And beyond doubt these institutions have exercised a great and salutary influence in stimulating the intellectual and literary activities of the nation. Many works of sterling merit in prose and verse have been called forth in the Welsh language by the prizes they have offered. And some productions, whose name and fame have travelled beyond the circle of mere Welsh celebrity, owe their existence to them—such as Miss Williams's collection of old Welsh melodies, mentioned in my last letter; Mr. John Thomas's *cantata* of " Llewellyn," produced for the Swansea Eisteddfod; Schultz's " Essay on the influence of Welsh Tradition upon the Literature of Germany, France, and Scandinavia"; and Stephens's work on " The Literature of the Kymry," an admirable volume, distinguished alike by sound judgment and solid learning. But more valuable still are the indirect effects they have produced, in diffusing through the whole country a spirit of literary and artistic emulation, which has acted as a powerful inducement to study and mental cultivation; for every town, and village, or neighbourhood has its own miniature Eisteddfod, where prizes are offered for the best essays and poems, the best singing and musical composi- tions. I dare say many of the productions offered on such occasions are crude and valueless enough; but the habit of application and research and the effort in com- position, however bungling and inexpert, are very far from being valueless.

In nothing, however, has the influence of the Eis- teddfodau been so powerful as in the impulse they have given to the study of music. The love of music has always been a passion with the Welsh people, and one of the pleasantest features in the rural life of the country, is the way in which the peasantry accompany their labour with singing. During harvest time especially the fields often ring with the sound of song and psalm, to which is sometimes added—a beautiful custom, to my feeling—the voice of prayer lifted in thanksgiving to the great Giver, while the workers stand or kneel amid the fragrant hay-swaths they have just cut, or under the golden sheaves of corn they have bound and stacked.

A century ago, from about 1750 to 1790, there came a period of decay as respects instrumental and vocal music in Wales. And as this synchronises pretty closely with the rise of Methodism, I have no doubt there was a considerable connection between the two things. Not that the leaders of that movement discouraged or ignored music. On the contrary, with great wisdom and skill, they pressed it into the service of religion, and nothing probably helped more to spread the sacred fire they had kindled than the hymns of the Rev. William Williams, of Pantycelin, one of the seceding clergymen who left the Church at that time, who was endowed with a rare genius for devotional poetry, and has produced some of the noblest hymns to be found in any language. But unhappily, in the dark days that preceded that era the sweet sounds of the mountain harp had been far too much associated with scenes of profane and riotous mirth, from which it became the aim, as it was the duty, of the religious reformers to wean the people. About this time, also, some of the most celebrated of the old minstrels and harpers—such as Edward Jones, Blind Parry, Will Hopkin, &c.—disappeared from the stage, leaving no immediate successors. And thus it happened that the cultivation of the old national music—at least, of the secular kind—fell into desuetude. Within the last forty years, however, the taste for music has revived and spread with wonderful rapidity, until it has overrun the whole face of the country, almost verifying the poetic hyperbole of one enthusiastic bard, who says—

Môr o gân yw Cymru i gyd,

E

That is,

All Wales is now one sea of song.

Among the quarrymen of the North Wales slate districts, n the neighbourhood of Llanidloes and Aberystwith, and among the ironworks of Glamorganshire and Monmouthshire, chorus-singing has reached a point of excellence hardly credible to those who only knew Wales twenty-five years ago. The singing of some of the choirs at Merthyr, Aberdare, Dowlais, Swansea, and Cardiff, may without discredit be brought into comparison with the best in London—excepting always Mr. Henry Leslie's—in point of delicacy, finish, and execution. This applies especially to the singing of the hill districts of South Wales. In that part of the country there are frequent performances of the " Messiah," " Creation," " Judas Maccabæus," etc. ; and I understand that Costa's " Naaman " is now (1866) in active rehearsal, and will be produced this spring.

Mr. Chorley, whose competency and honesty as a musical critic no one will call in question, and who has the reputation of being rather chary of his praises, heard some of these choirs at the Eisteddfod in Swansea in 1863. In an article from his pen which appeared in *All the Year Round* for October of the same year, he thus speaks of them :—

" The singing of the chorus was a great pleasure and astonishment. The power and the pleasure of co-operation have got hold of the men who come up from the mines or ride home from the forge on a grimy waggon along a tramway, in the midst of scoria or cinders, or work at trade in town, or at husbandry in country. The folk of Cornwall and Northumberland, so far as I know, are far less tuneful; and I do not fancy that the farm labourers of Kent or Warwickshire would trudge so far, or work so heartily, to get to a singing practice. The spirit of melody lies deep in the hearts of the Welsh. Their women have, as a race, very sweet, if not very strong, voices ; and recollecting as I do the far more experienced trebles of Bradford, Manchester, Norwich, and those we hear in London, I can credit these maids and matrons of Glamorganshire with admirable and prepossessing natural gifts. It is impossible to recall anything much more real and attractive than the sweet, zealous concord of the chorus in the charming old tunes which have been so well harmonised by Mr. John Thomas. One could swallow a column of titles as fantastic, &c., &c., for the sake of anything so real, so peculiar. Never could melodies, never chorus, have been more heartily relished."

But the noteworthy fact in respect to the choral societies of Wales is, that not only the members of the choir, but the chorus-masters are, without exception, amateurs, and nearly all working men, who have received no professional instruction whatever. The practices also have to be carried on without accompaniment of any kind.*

The fame of the musical genius of Wales has of late years spread far beyond the Principality. Welshmen are proud to claim as their countrymen such men as Mr. Brinley Richards and Mr. John Thomas. "The delicious national singing," as Mr. Chorley describes it, "of Miss Edith Wynne," is now well known in most parts of England. And Miss Edmonds, whom many of your readers have no doubt lately heard in London, was quietly taking her part in a choir at Swansea,

* For much of the information contained in this letter on the musical proficiency of the Welsh I am indebted to Dr. Evan Davies, of Swansea, a gentleman who in various ways has done more, perhaps, than any man living to promote a higher order of education among the working and middle classes of his countrymen.

E 2

within twelve months of the day on which she made
her appearance at Exeter Hall as first soprano in Mr.
Costa's "Naaman," on its first performance in London,
taking the part written originally for Patti, and sung by
her afterwards, but not to the absolute discredit, in
the comparison, of the little Welsh girl. It is not
every Welsh singer, however, that is directed by Providence to such accomplished teachers as Mr. and Mrs.
Sims Reeves.

There is another young Welshwoman, Miss Watts,
who, if she has her health, and is placed under wise
guidance, bids fair to reach a high place in the foremost ranks of the profession. She has already won
the £50 prize of the Royal Academy of Music. And
it is a remarkable illustration of the patriotic and
musical enthusiasm of the Welsh that last year a sum
of more than £500 was raised by concerts, to enable
her to pursue her musical education, by much the
larger part of which was contributed, not by the
wealthy, but by the working people of her native
district.

LETTER VII.

FREEDOM FROM CRIME IN WALES.

IN one of my former letters I stated that, since the fact
became established beyond the possibility of further dispute, that the great bulk of the inhabitants of Wales are
Dissenters, "an attempt had been made to discredit
the cause of Nonconformity by blackening the character
of the Welsh." When this was done, thirty-five years
ago, through the means of the Commissioners on Educa-

tion, I had the honour of standing up in this metropolis
to repel the aspersions that were then cast upon my
countrymen. There were many able writers and speakers
in Wales, of whom I may mention especially the late
Rev. Evan Jones, of Tredegar, an admirable man and a
true patriot, who rallied to the defence. But certainly
no more earnest and competent champion appeared in the
field than Sir Thomas Phillips. I have all the more
pleasure in acknowledging the great services by which,
on that occasion, this gentleman endeared himself to the
hearts of his compatriots, from the fact that he was a
zealous Churchman and, I believe, a Conservative. But
he was too genuine a lover of truth and of the land that
gave him birth, to connive at an attempt to snatch an
unfair advantage to his Church by the wholesale slander
of his countrymen—if, indeed, it is conceivable that any
Christian Church can derive advantage from representing
the people of whom it has had charge for three centuries,
as being utterly ignorant and depraved. Sir Thomas, in
his work entitled " Wales ; the Language, Social Condition, and Religious Opinions of the People," proved, by
an array of facts and of statistics derived from official
sources, that was absolutely overwhelming, and which no
one has ever refuted—or, so far as I know, attempted to
refute—that the morality of Wales, so far from being
lower, was very much higher than the average morality
of England.

When penning the sentence I have cited at the beginning of this letter, I did not expect that an attempt would
be made so soon again to revive the old exploded calumny.
But so it is. Mr. Bright having, in the debate on church-
rates, quoted some of the statistics given in one of my
former letters, as to the relative numbers of Churchmen
and Dissenters in the Principality, Mr. Gathorne Hardy
—discreetly, however, qualifying his statement with the

remark, " if I am rightly informed "—took upon himself to say that " much of the money employed for the erection of chapels in Wales is not given, but is lent on the mortgage of the pew-rents in those chapels. That is certainly a totally different thing from voluntary contributions for Church purposes. In the one case the money employed is derived from free and absolute gifts ; in the other, it is regarded purely as an investment ; and so profitable are these investments, yielding oftentimes as much as 7 per cent., that I am informed those who have lent their money are no sooner paid off than they transfer their capital to other and similar purposes."

Mr. Hardy was, of course, speaking according to his brief. Knowing nothing of Wales himself, he was only repeating what had been, probably, whispered in his ear by some ignorant Welsh member, of which class there are too many—ignorant, at least, of that which it most concerns them to know—the real habits and feelings of the people whom they profess to represent. But, most certainly, he was *not* " rightly informed." For, excepting the fact that in Wales, as in England, chapels, and, I suppose, churches too, are sometimes mortgaged when a sufficient sum cannot be raised at the time of building to defray the whole cost of erection, the above statement is a pure fiction. I will venture to say that no chapels have ever been built in Wales merely as a matter of profitable investment. They are built by the free contributions of the people, as they are needed, to supply the means of spiritual instruction. And as those requiring them are often a poor and never a wealthy population, they may be obliged to borrow a part of the money on the security of the building, and in some instances, for aught I know, if they fall into extortionate hands, to pay a high rate of interest upon it. But the chapel is always their own, vested in trust for their use, or for the use of the religious body to which they belong; nor do they rest satisfied until from their hard-earned savings they can pay off the mortgage, and leave no encumbrance on the house of their God.

But it evidently occurred in some more keen-eyed champion of the Church to reflect that, even assuming the case to be as Mr. Hardy represented it, such a showing did not much mend the matter, so far as the Church is concerned. For if, in addition to the maintenance of their ministers and schools, the current expenses of worship, and the repairs of the fabric, the people of Wales are willing to pay 7 per cent. on the money invested in the building, when they might use the parish church for nothing, surely this does not detract from the fervour of their Nonconformity, or the extent of the sacrifices they are willing to make for its sake. It would never do, therefore, to let the matter rest so. Accordingly, a writer in the *Press*, of the 10th of March, taking as his text Mr. Hardy's statement, itself utterly incorrect, develops and illustrates it in the following astonishing fashion After referring to Mr. Bright's figures, he adds :—

Mr. Bright did not stay to inquire into the particulars or the dimensions of these numerous edifices, nor to investigate the influences under which they are constructed. If he had done so, he would have revealed the workings of a system which he must have condemned as more oppressive and more inimical to true religious liberty than the infliction of church rates. Many of these buildings, it is well known, are built by the employers of labour in the various crowded localities and mining districts of Wales, or are held in mortgage by them for sums advanced for their construction; and consequently pains and penalties in many instances await those who refuse to frequent or encourage these chapels. Like the tally-shops, so long the curse of the manufacturing districts, these edifices are the properties of the masters, and a secret but sure tyranny is frequently exercised in promoting their support. There is another phase of the question suggested by these statistics worthy of the consideration of Mr. Bright. Let it be granted, to the fullest extent of his statement, that 75 per cent. of the population of Wales is placed for spiritual purposes

under dissent. Then a fair argument arises that the fruits of the
system are reflected in the character of the Welsh population.
But is not the Principality notoriously inferior in morality ? Are
not infanticide, illegitimate births, and affiliation cases in excess
of the average of any other portion of the United Kingdom ?

Here it will be seen that the old calumny as to the
immorality of the Welsh is revived. But before noticing
that, let me advert for a moment to the former part of
the statement relating to the influences under which, it is
alleged, the chapels are constructed and filled ; and let
me say at once, and with the utmost emphasis, that there
is absolutely not one word of truth in the whole of the
above tirade. Not only is it not true, but it is so gro-
tesquely unlike the truth, that one is astounded at the
ignorance or the audacity of the man who could venture
to perpetrate so outrageous a *canard*. It certainly will
be news to the people of Wales when they learn from the
revelations of this oracle that they are Nonconformists,
not from choice, but because they are driven, under
heavy pains and penalties, into the chapels built for them
by their masters. Why, Sir, "the masters," whether
that term is employed in reference to the employers of
labour in the mining districts, or to the landowners in
the agricultural districts, are almost without exception
Churchmen—and many of them very bigoted Churchmen, too—who vex their righteous souls not a little, not
with the unlawful deeds, but with the Nonconformist
proclivities of the people. They would no more think of
building a Dissenting chapel than they would of building
a synagogue for Satan. Nay, more, some of them, at
least, as I may have occasion to show hereafter, taking
advantage of their position as owners of property, do all
in their power to embarrass and obstruct the people in
their effort to build schools and places of worship for
themselves. There is, indeed, much pressure used by
the "masters" in Wales, but most assuredly that

pressure is not in favour of the chapel. In short, the facts are as nearly as possible the precise converse in every respect of what the *Press* states.

On the other point—the alleged immorality of the people of Wales—I accept the challenge of this writer. And, first of all, I will deal with the question of crime in the Principality. I have the "Judicial Statistics" of 1864 before me, from which I learn that the whole number of persons committed in England during that year was 122,589, or one to every 155 of the population. The number committed in Wales was 4,417, or 1 to every 252 of the population. But then, of the 4,417 committed in Wales, there were :—

Natives of England .	. . . . .	1,006
„ Ireland .	. . . .	846
„ Scotland .	. . . . .	78
„ The Colonies and East Indies.	.	135
Persons whose birthplace was unknown .	.	29
		2,094

Thus it will be seen that the proportion of criminals to the population in Wales is 44 per cent. less than in England, while of those criminals who disgrace the Principality nearly one-half are not natives.

Still more remarkable is the result when we come to look to the number of persons committed for trial on some of the more serious order of offences. Thus, those committed on a charge of murder were—in England, 67, or 1 to every 282,902 of the population; in Wales, 3, or 1 to every 370,902. Those committed on the charge of attempts at murder were—in England, 34; in Wales, none. Those committed on the charge of manslaughter were—in England, 217, or 1 to every 87,347 of the population; in Wales, 6, or 1 to every 186,963.

So, when we examine the number of convictions, the same, or nearly the same, disproportion exists. I cannot

tell the editor of the *Press* how many persons were convicted of infanticide in Wales in 1864, because that class
of crime is not entered separately, but comes, I suppose,
under the general designation of "murder." But I can
tell him how many were convicted of murder in Wales
in 1864—namely, *one*, a number which, I hope, he will
admit could not include *very* many cases of infanticide.

But even these statistics, striking as they are, give but
an imperfect idea of the paucity of serious crimes in
Wales. The editor of one of the Welsh periodicals
stated a few months ago that, but for the foreign tramps
that infested the country, the gaols in some of the
counties in Wales might really be almost shut up. I
wrote to ask him how he substantiated so startling an
allegation. He answered by sending me the following
summary taken from the *North Wales Chronicle* of all the
criminal business done at the Midsummer assizes of
1865, in four out of the six counties of North Wales :—

MONTGOMERYSHIRE.—Setting fire to a stack, Henry
Johnson (an Englishman) ; stealing a pair of boots,
William Griffith ; obtaining goods under false pretences,
Edward Beedle (an Englishman) ; forgery, Henry John-
son (an Englishman).

MERIONETHSHIRE.—Stealing a pair of boots, Edward
Haynes (an Englishman) and John Harris—Haynes
acquitted, Harris sentenced to three months ; rape,
Edward Evans—charge dismissed.

CARNARVONSHIRE.—Stealing 12s. 6d., William Smith
(an Englishman) ; John Jones, assault on a girl—charge
dismissed.

ANGLESEY.—Lord Chief Justice Cockburn thus addressed the grand jury :—" Gentlemen of the grand jury,
—I must express my congratulations to you that the Principality of Wales, and especially the county of Anglesey,
represent this year again the purity of conduct, the good

morals, and the honesty of purpose that have so long distinguished the inhabitants of the Principality, and I have the pleasure to inform you that there is not a single prisoner for trial at these assizes, or, as far as I am aware, any presentments for the grand jury to make. This is a happy state of things, which has existed for some time in your Principality, and we all trust that the freedom from crime which has so long distinguished Welshmen may continue to do so for a long time to come. Gentlemen, if you have no presentment of your own to make, I shall have great pleasure in discharging you on this occasion, with the thanks of the county for your services." The grand jury retired, and immediately returned into the court, when the foreman said, "I am happy to say we have no presentments to make." After they were discharged, the High Sheriff, addressing his lordship, said, " My lord, as high sheriff of this county, there being not a single prisoner for trial, I have very great pleasure, in accordance with ancient custom, in presenting you with a pair of white gloves." His lordship returned thanks, and said " they were all aware and rejoiced in the purity of the morals of the people of this country."

My informant adds that he had not the particulars of the Denbighshire assizes at hand, but that there were only three or four petty cases, of no importance whatever. I have ascertained that at Carmarthen there were at that assize only three prisoners for trial.

At the same assize Mr. Justice Shee thus addressed the grand jury at Cardiff:—

" I am happy to be the bearer of the Queen's commission to this prosperous and well-ordered country, and I thank you for your numerous attendance. I have now been in the discharge of the duty of my office for two years in the Principality; and as yet, though I have

visited three counties, only six persons have been convicted before me, so that, if my experience were to go no
further, I should be in the condition to say that the inhabitants of the Principality of Wales set a most excellent example to the rest of her Majesty's subjects."

And while I am writing this, a Welsh paper comes to
hand stating that Mr. Justice Blackburn has just held
the Spring assizes at Cardigan. In charging the grand
jury, he said :—

" At this assize I may almost congratulate you upon
having nothing to do. It is, in fact, the case, that the
county itself has furnished no business for these assizes."

There was only one case to be tried—that of two
English tramps for stealing from a dwelling-house, who
were sentenced to eight months' imprisonment. I hope
these testimonies of her Majesty's judges will be of some
account in the estimation of the *Press*.

These learned gentlemen, the judges, coming down
from England to preside at the assizes in Wales, struck
with this surprising absence of crime, and from their in-
acquaintance with the inner life of the country, being
unable to account for it in any other way, have usually
betaken themselves to complimenting the grand jury,
assuring them that the virtue of the people was, no
doubt, owing to their having a resident gentry among
them. I should think the gentlemen thus complimented
must find it rather difficult not to laugh in each other's
faces while listening to these eulogies, so perfectly must
they be aware how little any influence of theirs has to do
with the matter. It is quite certain that, if the gentry
lived altogether, as many of them do half their time, in
Bath, or Cheltenham, or London, or on the Continent, it
would not make the slightest difference in the conduct of
the Welsh people. The influence which has made them
so orderly, moral, and law-abiding, must be sought else-

where than in the abodes of the gentry. It must be sought in the four or five thousand chapels and churches, where a pure Gospel is preached every Sunday round the year. It must be sought in the Sunday-schools spread throughout the country, with their 40,000 voluntary teachers, where the mass of the people have their minds and hearts permèated with the great principles of Christian doctrine and morality. I had intended to have discussed in this letter the other question referred to in the extract from the *Press*—that of illegitimacy in Wales. But I have already occupied so much of your space, that I must defer it till next week.

LETTER VIII.

THE CHARGE OF EXCESS IN ILLEGITIMACY BROUGHT AGAINST WALES.

THERE is an animal haunting some of the less inhabited parts of North America bearing a name as unsavoury as its nature, which has the power of emitting a fluid of such intolerable fœtor that it nearly suffocates man and beast that come within its range. And, what is still worse, this noisome stench is all but indelible. Once it taints a piece of furniture or a garment it is next to impossible to be rid of it while a splinter or a shred of the article remains. No amount of washing or scrubbing, or exposure to the air can cleanse, nor can all the perfumes of Arabia sweeten, the thing it has touched. Calumny seems to have the same tenacious quality of clinging for ever to any object that has once been polluted by its obscene breath.

We have a striking illustration of this in the pertinacity with which the charge of immorality, especially as respects the relation of the sexes, has been and is reiterated against the Welsh people. How it originated it is difficult to say, but it is certain that the reports of the Commissioners on Education, in 1847-8, served to give it more weight, and a wider currency than it ever had before. It is a cruel thing that persons clothed with official prestige should, through ignorance, rashness, and credulity, have the power to brand with lasting infamy the character of a whole people. It is impossible to exaggerate the wrong which those Blue-books have done to the reputation of the Principality ; for, as documents promulgated under the sanction of the Government, they are still referred to with unquestioning faith by writers who have no means of knowing that their correctness and credibility have ever been called in question. All Welshmen who have crossed the border are well aware how, through their means, a notion is still widely prevalent in England that the Principality is, especially as respects the sin of unchastity, in a grossly and exceptionally depraved condition. It is alleged that the habits of the peasantry are on this point worse than in any part of the kingdom—that, in the language of one of the witnesses cited by the Commissioners, though he, I am convinced, erred from ignorance and not from malice, "the number of illegitimate children, when compared with England, is astounding" ; or in the words of the *Press*, cited in my last letter, that "the Principality is notoriously inferior in morality, and that infanticide, illegitimate births, and affiliation cases are in excess of the average of any other portion of the United Kingdom." These imputations have been again and again refuted by facts and statistics of unimpeachable authenticity and accuracy. But there are people who seem to take a prurient delight in dwelling on such unclean exaggerations, and to surrender the belief in them with the greatest possible reluctance. I must, therefore, once more lay the evidence before your readers to prove that this impeachment of the character of my countrymen and countrywomen is, in the grossly exaggerated sense in which it is usually made, without foundation. I do not deny that unchastity exists in Wales. I do not deny that it exists there in a measure that grieves and distresses all true lovers of their country. But I do very confidently deny that it exists there in such form and degree as to make it—as was alleged by the Commissioners, and is confidently repeated by the slavish retailers of their scandal—" the peculiar vice of the Principality." Nay, I believe I can show that, though falling lamentably below the standard of the Divine law, it has the right to claim credit for superior purity as compared with most other parts of the kingdom.

In investigating such a charge as this, it is only fair to remember that there are other forms of unchastity besides that which expresses itself by illegitimacy, such as prostitution, adultery, concubinage, cohabitation without marriage, and others of a still more occult though not less deadly nature. And communities in which these notoriously abound have small right to lift their eyes to Heaven in sanctimonious disgust, and to thank God they are not like other men, even though it could be proved that the former evil happens to be less rife among them. Now, it is only on the first count of this indictment that anybody pretends to arraign the Welsh people as being specially guilty, while all who have any acquaintance with the country declare with one accord that, as respects the other forms of the evil enunciated above, they are a singularly exemplary community.

Let us see, however, how the matter stands in reference

even to that particular point to which the accusation more emphatically applies. It is a curious thing
that men should have hazarded such wild assertions as
they have done as to the extent of illegitimacy in Wales,
when the means were at hand from which they might
have obtained the most accurate and precise information
—in the " Annual Reports " of the Registrar-General.
As an example of the reckless manner in which the fair
fame of a whole country has been trifled with, take the
following statement—made by one of the Commissioners
to whom I have so often referred—namely, " That the
proportion of illegitimate children in North Wales shows
an excess of 12·3 per cent. on the calculated average of
all England and Wales in the year 1842 upon the like
number of registered births," the fact being, as the
official documents show, that the average of North
Wales for that very year was only 7·5 per cent.
altogether !

But to return from this digression, I take the Registrar-
General's Report for 1863. The whole country, exclusive
of the metropolis, is divided, for the purposes of the
Registration Act, into ten districts. Of these Wales and
Monmouthshire form one. The proportion of illegitimate
children for every 100 children born in all these dis-
tricts is as follows, to which I have added those of
Scotland :—

Scotland (in 1862)		9·7
Northern District		8·7
North Midland District . , . .		8·3
Yorkshire ,, ...		8·2
Eastern ,, ...		8·2
North Western ,, ...		7·2
West Midland ,, ...		7·1
WELSH ,, ...		6·9
South Midland ,, ...		6·5
South Western ,.		6·08
South Eastern ,, ...		5·6

From which it will appear that Wales, so far from being

at the top of the list, is the lowest but three of all the divisions. But there is another way of showing this matter, suggested by the Registrar-General in his Fourteenth Annual Report. " It must not be immediately assumed," he says, " as has been sometimes done, in comparing the counties of England and Wales, that the relative morality of the population is expressed by these numbers." He then points out the child-bearing ages of women as being between fifteen and fifty-five, and principally between twenty and forty, and shows in a table the number of women married and unmarried in each county at the two divisions of ages, as ascertained by the last census then preceding, and the births of children in each class, and the proportional number of children to women. The following extract is given from that table :—

Registration Divisions.	Proportions of Births in Wedlock to 100 Married Women.		Proportions of Births out of Wedlock to 100 Unmarried Women and Widows.	
	Under the Age of 40.	Under the Age of 55.	Of the Age of 28—40.	Of the Age of 15—55.
England	35·197	22·470	3·365	1·715
London.	30·657	20·420	1·500	·821
South Eastern counties	35·023	21·920	3·064	1·860
South Midland counties	35·701	22·400	3·946	1·944
Eastern counties . .	34·572	21·463	4·934	2·462
South Western counties	36·677	22·020	2·735	1·396
West Midland counties	35·531	22·597	3·707	1·855
North Midland counties	35·978	22·298	4·494	2·213
North West counties .	36·123	23·903	3·757	1·936
Yorkshire	36·608	23·742	4·101	2·018
Northern counties . .	37·781	24·510	4·254	2·086
Monmouthshire and Wales .	36·143	22·344	3·517	1·791

Upon this the Registrar-General remarks :—

Excluding London from view, as the returns are probably imperfect, it may be inferred that, generally, the unmarried women in the counties south of the Thames, comprising the old Saxon

F

population, have few illegitimate children ; Wales stands next in
the scale.   The West Midland, the North Western, and the South
Midland counties, covering the area of the ancient Mercia, present
less favourable results ; while in Yorkshire, the Northern counties,
the North Midland counties, and particularly the Eastern
counties, covering the area of the ancient Danish population, the
number of illegitimate children is exceedingly great.

But when we come to compare Wales with many of the
separate counties in England, the falsity of the *Press's*
assertion that, as respects illegitimate births, the Principality is in " excess of the average of any other portion
of the United Kingdom," becomes still more strikingly
apparent.   This will be seen by the following table :—

Wales	6·9
Bedfordshire	7·1
Oxfordshire	7·3
Suffolk	7·9
Herefordshire	8·7
Lincolnshire	8·9
Nottinghamshire	9·1
Westmoreland	9·2
North Riding	9·6
Shropshire	10·1
Norfolk	11·3
Cumberland	12·0

But the amount of bastardy is no accurate measure of
the chastity, far less of the general morality, of a people.
No stronger evidence of this can be desired than is
afforded by the fact that the per-centage of illegitimacy
is smaller in London than in any part of the kingdom,
and that it is smallest of all in those districts of London
that are notoriously the lowest in reputation.   Thus we
find that while the proportion of illegitimate births in all
London is 4·4 per cent., in Whitechapel it is only 3·3 ;
in Poplar, 3·1 ; in Bethnal Green, 2·6 ; in St. Luke's,
2·1.   No one will imagine that this paucity of illegitimate children is owing to superior purity of the districts named.   It is owing, unhappily, to a far less
creditable cause, to the prevalence of the various other

forms of incontinence previously referred to ; and in regard to those I believe the Welsh people will compare favourably with any community in the world. " Conjugal infidelity," says Dr. Rees, of Swansea, in an able paper on this subject, which he read at one of the Social Science meetings of the Eisteddfod held in that town in 1861, " is of comparatively rare occurrence in the Principality. Many large districts of the country might bo named in which not one instance of adultery has been found during a whole generation. The sacredness of the marriage covenant and the enormity of the sin of adultery are happily regarded and felt throughout the nation."

On the subject of prostitution, we have the means of making an approximate comparison. Under the head of " Police," in the " Judicial Statistics," there is a return of the number of prostitutes in the various counties of England and Wales. It is obviously imperfect, and imperfect in a way that must be greatly to the disadvantage of the more scattered population. For while in the small towns and villages every person whose character is at all even suspected must be perfectly well known to the police, in the dense population of large towns, like London and Liverpool, many such must of necessity escape observation. But let us take these returns as they are. I must, however, premise one explanation. It must be remembered that the charge I am rebutting is brought against the Welsh people, the inhabitants of what may be called Wales Proper, and more emphatically against those residing in the agricultural districts. It is of North Wales, which is almost wholly of that character, that the Commissioners say, " There is one vice (unchastity) which is flagrant throughout North Wales, and remains unchecked by any instrument of civilisation." It is of the "peasantry"

F 2

of Cardiganshire, Breconshire, Carmarthenshire, &c.,
that the same authorities allege that "they are almost
universally unchaste." When on the subject of prostitution, therefore, it is with these districts of the country
that the comparison must be made. Not but that it is
sufficiently favourable to Wales, even if the whole
country were taken indiscriminately. But the large
towns of Glamorganshire, such as Cardiff, Swansea,
Merthyr, &c., have long ceased to be distinctively Welsh.
"There," says Sir Thomas Phillips, who lived in or near
that district, "are found large numbers of Englishmen
and Irishmen, many of them driven by crime or want,
and characterised by much that is lawless and unrestrained." Indeed, in the great ports of the above
county there is a singularly promiscuous population,
including persons, especially of the sailor class, not only
from England and Ireland, but from almost every nation
under heaven. A striking proof of this is afforded by
the fact, that out of all the committals in Glamorganshire, in 1864, considerably more than one-half were
foreigners, that is, not natives of the Principality. It
would be obviously absurd, therefore, to include this
mixed multitude under the designation of "the Welsh
people."

Confining myself, therefore, to Wales Proper, but
omitting Glamorganshire, I find the result of the returns
respecting prostitution is this, that while in England
prostitutes bear the proportion of 1 to every 364 women,
being ·27 per cent. on the whole female population, in
Wales they bear the proportion of 1 to every 1,548
women, or ·064 per cent. of the female population. There
is another significant fact that may be mentioned in connection with this subject. In the "Judicial Statistics"
there is a return of "Brothels and Houses of Ill Fame,"
of which there are 7,092 in England and Wales. But

the portion allotted to Wales, omitting Glamorganshire,
is as follows :—Anglesey, not one ; Cardiganshire, not
one ; Merionethshire, not one ; Radnorshire, not one ;
Flintshire, 1 ; Breconshire, 3 ; Denbighshire, 4 ; Mont-
gomeryshire, 7 ; Carnarvonshire, 10 ; Carmarthenshire,
11 ; Pembrokeshire, I am sorry to say, 45. But it is a
very noteworthy fact, of which those must make what
they can who maintain that the salvation of Wales
depends on its forgetting Welsh and adopting the English
language, that every one of those houses of ill fame in
Pembrokeshire are in the purely English part of the
county—Pembroke, Tenby, and Haverfordwest.

As to the attempt to connect the alleged immorality of
Wales with the prevalence of Dissent, I have one or two
words of not unfriendly caution to give to our Church
friends. They will find this a most dangerous and
double-edged weapon to wield. For if the fact that in
Wales, where Nonconformity predominates, 6·9 per cent.
of the births are illegitimate proves that Dissenting
teaching is immoral, then, of course, by perfect parity of
reasoning, the fact that in Cumberland, where the
Church of England predominates, 12·0 per cent. of the
births are illegitimate, proves that the teaching of the
Church is nearly twice as immoral as that of Dissent.
But there is another much more serious aspect of the
imputation. Those who make it know well enough, or
might know if they chose to inquire, that the Dissenters
in Wales, as in England, teach and preach nothing but
the doctrines and duties of Christianity. The only book
that is taught by their 30,000 or 40,000 Sunday-school
teachers is the Bible. There is not one, I will venture
to say, of the upwards of 3,000 Dissenting pulpits in
Wales where the pure and lofty morality of the Gospel
is not habitually and earnestly enforced. Nay, more, as
I can bear witness from frequent observation, it is

brought to bear upon the current vices of society, and emphatically upon the particular vice of which I have been treating in this letter, with a plainness of application and a directness and solemnity of appeal which would throw half the fashionable congregations of London into hysterics. If, therefore, teaching of this sort produces an immoral people, it is clear that the indictment lies, not against Dissent, but against Christianity.

LETTER IX.

LIBERALITY OF THE WELSH PEOPLE.

In my last two letters I endeavoured, not unsuccessfully, I hope, to vindicate the Welsh people from certain imputations that have been cast upon their character on matters of personal and social morality. But something more than this should be done. It is not enough to prove that they are not worse than many, probably better than most, of their fellow-subjects in other parts of the kingdom as respects their freedom from the grosser forms of crime and vice. A community whose religious privileges and professions are so ample ought to be able to show some fruits of positive and practical virtue. But it is not easy to find any tangible test of this. You cannot formulise into a schedule the quiet household virtues of a people.

> The charities that soothe, and heal, and bless,
> Are scattered at the feet of men like flowers;

and their silent beauty and fragrance can only be discerned by those who move familiarly among the scenes

where they flourish and bloom. I do sincerely believe
that these may be found, in no stinted measure, to adorn
the humble homes of multitudes of my countrymen.
But they are things that cannot be represented by
statistical calculations and averages.

There is, however, one standard by which we may
pretty fairly appraise the practical influence which a
people's faith has produced on their character, that is,
the degree in which they are ready to make exertions
and sacrifices for purposes of religion and charity. And
I think the inhabitants of the Principality need not
shrink from being brought to this standard. I have
already referred, in a former letter, to the more than
3,000 chapels, most of them built or rebuilt within the
last fifty years, which attest the extent of their liberality.
Many of these are, no doubt, very plain structures, but
not so as to be at all out of harmony with the abodes of
those for whose use they are intended. On the contrary,
plain as the chapel often is, it is usually the most
capacious and stately building in the neighbourhood. It
is not easy to form an estimate of what these places of
worship have cost, for a large proportion of the contributions are, in many places, given in kind. For instance,
the proprietor of a quarry will allow the stones necessary
for the building to be taken without charge. The farmers
will send their horses and carts to carry the materials
without charge. And sometimes working men will, by
working extra hours, give their labour for nothing, or at
a reduced rate. The amount of actual money, therefore,
required is frequently not large. But if we assume them
to have cost no more than £500 each on an average, this
will give more than a million and a half expended in
about fifty years. And while on this point I must be
allowed to quote a few sentences from a letter just
written to me by a gentleman at Dolgelley, which will

throw some light upon what appears to have puzzled
Mr. Gathorne Hardy and others :—

As for Mr. Hardy's remark (he says), that chapels are built for
the sake of the excessive interest which the money invested in
them brings to speculators, I can only say that, in this part of the
country, at least, it is so far otherwise, that money advanced on
chapels is usually without any interest at all. In the district of
the Festiniog Quarries (the quarries in which Lord Palmerston
was so large a shareholder) the people manage matters in this
way. When it is determined to build a new chapel in any neighbourhood, to cost, say, £2,000, the members of the church and
congregation form themselves into a society, and agree to sub-
scribe monthly, while the building is in course of erection, a sum
varying from 1s. to £5, according to their ability and inclination,
as a building fund, which is lent upon the chapel without interest.
When the building is opened, they then contribute smaller sums
monthly towards the gradual extinction of the debt, which is not
very long in being cancelled altogether.

It is difficult to ascertain with precise accuracy what
is the amount which the Nonconformists in Wales raise
annually for the various objects of a religious and
benevolent character in which they are interested. I
have two estimates, from two gentlemen who have paid
considerable attention to the subject. One says :—" The
Nonconformists of Wales contribute for all purposes—
including schools—about a quarter of a million of pounds
annually." The other says : " I have often attempted
to make a calculation of the aggregate sum raised for all
religious objects by the Dissenters of Wales, and my
impression is that, including the extra efforts made for
the erection of chapels and schools, it amounts to at
least £300,000 a year."

To understand the full significance of this fact, it must
be borne in mind that the gentry, and, as a rule, the
wealthy classes generally, are Churchmen ; so that these
sums are derived almost entirely from the middle and
working classes. It must be also remembered that all
this is paid by way of voluntary offering, in addition to
what is extracted from them by compulsory exaction for

the support of the Establishment. The revenues of the Established Church in Wales have been thus estimated :—

Incomes of the four bishops	£17,100
Deans and canons	10,000
1,050 parochial benefices, averaging £220 each	231,000
Charities under the management of the clergy for the support of schools, &c.	23,931
Church-rates and voluntary contributions in aid of Church-rates, according to Parliamentary paper No. 4, 1859	24,648
Burial and other fees, value of glebe houses, salaries of the archdeacons, chaplains in the prisons, union workhouses, &c., may be estimated at	21,000
Total	£327,679

So that the annual amount raised by the Welsh Nonconformists of their own free will does not fall far short of all the revenues of the Church imposed upon them by authority, but whose services they decline to accept.

I may mention some other facts illustrating the vigour and fruitfulness of the voluntary principle in Wales. It is now, I think, about twenty-five years since the Calvinistic Methodists of South Wales re-opened, as an institution for training young men for the ministry, Lady Huntingdon's College at Trevecca. But before doing so they raised a sum of £10,000 for repairing the building and providing funds for the institution, which is now about to be augmented by an addition of £20,000 to be raised during the next four years. Within the last five years the same body in North Wales have subscribed no less a sum than £35,000 for the erection and endowment of a college for the same purpose at Bala.

About thirty years ago the Welsh Independents determined by a concerted effort to clear their chapels of the debts by which they were at that time encumbered. And in a short time, with some help from England, they raised some £25,000 for the purpose. In the year 1862 the same denomination, by way of commemorating the Nonconformist ejection two centuries before, started a fund to spread over five years for building a new college at Brecon, and for erecting chapels in destitute localities, or aiding in liquidating the debts upon those previously erected, and from the progress already made it is confidently anticipated that before the end of 1867 it will amount to £30,000. On the same occasion the Baptist body, not so numerous nor so wealthy, began a fund for somewhat similar purposes. At the outset they modestly limited their aim to £4,000 or £5,000. But already nearly £14,000 has been promised, and it is believed that before the end of the prescribed period the sum will considerably exceed that. There are no fewer than seven Nonconformist colleges supported in the Principality, two by the Calvinistic Methodists, three by the Independents (one of them partially aided from the Presbyterian Fund Board in London), and three by the Baptists.

But while thus attending to their own requirements, the Welsh people by no means neglect the claims of others. They contribute more bountifully to the Bible Society than any part of the kingdom, according to the number of the population. In the last report of that excellent institution (1865) the committee say :—

It is with feelings of peculiar interest that the committee turn to Wales, and observe that there is no diminution in the substantial proofs so long afforded of hearty attachment to the society. The liberality evinced in the annual remittance of large free contributions from the auxiliaries is truly surprising, when the limited amount of the population and other circumstances are concerned, and the same scale of liberality practised in England would replenish the resources of the society to an extent far in advance of any point hitherto reached.

The Calvinistic Methodists have a Foreign Missionary Society of their own, and support missions in India and in Brittany, the latter field of labour having been selected for the very natural reason that the Bretons are the near kindred of the Welsh, a colony driven from their island home to seek refuge in France when the people of Wales were sorely pressed by the Saxon invaders, it is supposed, about the fifth or sixth century. The Episcopalians, the Independents, the Baptists, and the Wesleyan Methodists remit their contributions for the same purpose to the societies which represent their repective bodies in London. Towards most of the other objects which engage the attention and sympathies of Christians in England, such as the diffusion of the Gospel on the Continent and in the Colonies, the conversion of the Jews, the religious instruction of sailors, &c., the Welsh Nonconformists contribute their quota.

I must now say a few words on the question of popular education in Wales. About thirty years ago the friends of the Church in Wales, evidently in despair of luring back the adult population within the ecclesiastical fold whence they had strayed, betook themselves very zealously to the work of day-school education, with the avowed object of using it as an instrument of proselytism. When the Committee of Council began to make grants for the erection of schools, many of the Dissenters in Wales had strong scruples, not without good reason in my judgment, against applying for a share of those grants. But our Church friends are never troubled with much scruple when public money is to be obtained, and in the Principality there was a perfect rush of claimants among the clergy and gentry for aid to build national schools. For several years this was accorded with lavish profusion, and with very little inquiry beyond the bare allegations of the applicants. No one, perhaps, could have found much fault with Churchmen for so eagerly seizing the advantage placed within their reach by the Government, even though their zeal for education was prompted by no higher a motive than the wish to pervert the children of Dissenters from the faith of their fathers—if only they had used their advantage with anything like fairness.

But they used it with the utmost unfairness. Large grants were obtained from the Committee of Council for the erection of church schools in districts where there were absolutely no children, or next to none, but those of Dissenting parents; and in these schools, built—in great part—with money drawn from the general taxation of the country, the learning of the Church Catechism, and attendance on Church services, were rigidly enforced. The hardship of this was all the greater, as there are no people in the world who have a stronger repugnance than the Welsh Nonconformists to the doctrine of baptismal regeneration so emphatically taught in the Church Catechism. A very striking illustration of this was afforded some fourteen or fifteen years ago. Mr. J. Bowstead, one of her Majesty's Inspectors of Schools, on visiting South Wales for the purposes of his office, was very much struck with the practical anomaly of National Schools of the strictest order planted in the midst of exclusively Dissenting populations. And having soon ascertained the feelings of the people on the subject, he had the courage to put a paragraph in his report, in which he stated that such schools were ill-adapted for the Principality, inasmuch as the parents cherished the painful belief that in them their children "ran the risk of being imbued with catechisms and formularies which they themselves hold in a sort of abhorrence." Six years after the appearance of this report the Bishop of St. David's (Dr. Thirlwall), in one of his charges, peremptorily denied the correctness of Mr. Bowstead's statements, and characterised them as "absurd exaggerations." No one doubted for an instant that the Bishop spoke in perfect good faith, but it is the misfortune of men in his high position that they have little opportunity of coming into direct contact with the mass of the people among whom they dwell. Nor must it be denied that there were

appearances which lent considerable plausibility to the
opinion he expressed as to the indifference with which
Dissenting parents saw their children taught the Church
Catechism. But when Mr. Bowstead found his statement challenged from such a quarter, he felt that he was
bound to make it good by the adduction of adequate
evidence. He accordingly addressed a circular, briefly
stating the case, to nearly three hundred persons in
South Wales and Monmouthshire, including persons of
every religious denomination and of every grade in life,
asking them if he had misrepresented the feelings of the
Welsh Dissenters as respects the teaching of the Catechism to their children. The response, as anyone who
had the slightest acquaintance with the country might
have anticipated, was overwhelming in the unanimity
and emphasis with which it ratified Mr. Bowstead's
opinion. This assuredly arose from no prejudice against
the Bishop of St. David's personally, who is respected
and honoured by all classes in the Principality, Dissenters as well as Churchmen.

It may be asked if such were the feelings of Dissenting
parents in Wales, how came it to pass that they sent
their children to such schools? The answer is, that
there exists among the ·Welsh people an extreme eager-
ness for education; and as the National school was
often the only one to be found in a neighbourhood,
rather than forfeit altogether the advantages of the
general instruction afforded there, they suffered their
children to swallow the obnoxious formulary, hoping by
antidotes applied at home to counteract what they
deemed the dangerous errors it inculcated. But what
shall we say to their tempters? Must it not be a matter
of endless astonishment that honourable and religious
men can reconcile it to their consciences to seduce, and
sometimes coerce, little children into repeating, day by

day, what they must know perfectly well is on *their* lips
a deliberate falsehood; and that not on a point of trivial
import, but on one which many of the catechists themselves acknowledge, and even emphatically maintain, lies
at the basis of their Church's whole system of teaching?
The case was so forcibly put in an article which appeared
a few weeks ago in the *Times*, probably from the pen of
one who has had personal experience of this matter, that
I must ask permission to insert a short extract here. It
was written *à propos* of a debate in Convocation on the
" Conscience Clause " :—

> There is found everywhere a tradition of some fanatical sect
> once a year sacrificing a child, with circumstances and rites more
> or less horrible. On Wednesday the victim was brought into the
> Lower House of Convocation, in the form of an imaginary boy or
> girl, of Dissenting parents, asking admission to the village school,
> with its neighbours and playfellows. Its parents are Baptists,
> and its baptism has accordingly been deferred till it could under-
> stand something of the matter. Of course, it is not in a condition
> to say that its name was given to it by its godfathers and god-
> mother, for it has none; *and as the whole of the Catechism has been
> ingeniously constructed to hang on that one reply, the child can have
> nothing to say to it.* In other respects it cannot fall into the
> usual routine of the Church of England education, though it may
> easily know more of the Bible than its school-fellows. To admit
> the child, and to compel it, or even to encourage it, to join in a
> course of instruction, vitiated in its case by a fundamental
> untruth, is an hypocrisy, a fraud, and an oppression. In the
> slack old times many clergy and many parents tolerated such a
> practice, thinking it mattered little one way or the other, and the
> child got an education. But conscientious, reflecting parents did
> not like it, and even if they would have borne it themselves, or
> were not strong enough to fight their own battles, their religious
> teachers put them up to resist; and there was a resistance. The
> Dissenters made common cause, and claimed the benefit of the
> village school, assisted by public money, without being compelled
> to take the Church Catechism into the bargain. Hence the
> " Conscience Clause," or rather the system of indulgence expressed
> in the phrase, and of which it is the type.

But in Wales the promoters of the illiberal system of
education have in the main failed of their purpose. This
is acknowledged in a very lugubrious pamphlet, published

some years ago, by the Rev. Canon Williams, of Bangor, in the form of a letter to the bishop of that diocese, wherein he says that "there are few subjects of regret more generally alluded to, in Wales at least, than the failure of the National schools as a means of attaching the pupils, in after life, to the Church." Meanwhile, the Dissenters have not been idle in the matter of day-school education. More than twenty years ago I had the pleasure, in conjunction with many abler and more influential men, of taking part in an educational movement which led to very considerable results, especially in South Wales. A normal school was established at Brecon, and thence transferred to Swansea, which for several years was conducted with admirable efficiency. Owing to a combination of untoward circumstances, it has now ceased to exist; but it lived long enough tò give a most valuable impulse to the cause of education in the Principality. Dr. Davies, who was at its head, has said recently, "During the last twenty years I may say that probably between 300 and 400 really good schools have been started in South Wales, which is the part I know most intimately, where the ordinary subjects, such as English grammar and arithmetic, are very well taught." It is not at all meant to be implied that these are all Dissenting schools, though I have no doubt a large proportion of them owe their existence, directly or indirectly, to the influence of the movement alluded to.

In North Wales, also, the work of promoting a liberal system of education has, within the last few years, been carried on with remarkable vigour and success. A normal college has been opened at Bangor, towards the establishment of which the Welsh people have contributed nearly £12,000, which is now in full and efficient operation. A gentleman, who has himself been a main agent in this good work, says, in a letter to me :—

We have now 215 British schools in Wales, all of which have been established within the last twenty years, and that by the exertions of what is called "the people," with little, *very* little, assistance from the gentry. There are, indeed, a few honourable exceptions. The same fact is also true as regards the maintenance of these institutions. The contributions of the public towards the building fund of Bangor College amounted to £11,600, by far the largest portion of which came out of plebeian pockets.

LETTER X.

POLITICAL CONDITION OF WALES—STATE OF THE REPRESENTATION.

HAVING dwelt at some length on the religious, moral, and social condition of Wales, I propose in my two or three remaining letters to say something as to its political condition.

It is now more than three centuries since Wales became politically incorporated with England by being admitted to share in its system of Parliamentary representation. Up to that time the English Government had attempted to subdue the Welsh by force of arms and by oppressive penal legislation. But this masterful policy failed utterly and ignominiously, as it richly deserved to fail. "An old and haughty nation, proud in arms," as Milton describes them, the inhabitants of " gwyllt Walia " continued among their mountain fastnesses fierce, unconquerable, defiant. But what violence could not do, justice and conciliation speedily accomplished. Burke in his great speech on " Conciliation with America," cites the case of Wales as a cardinal example of the folly and impotence of the one system of rule, and the wisdom and virtue of the other. After describing the various measures taken "to subdue the fierce spirit of the Welsh by all sorts of rigorous laws," he adds :—

But all this while Wales rid this country like an incubus; it was an unprofitable and oppressive burthen; and an Englishman travelling in that country could not go six yards from the high road without being murdered. It was not until after two hundred years discovered that, by an eternal law, Providence had decreed vexation to violence, and poverty to rapine. Our ancestors did, however, at length open their eyes to the ill husbandry of injustice. Accordingly, in the 27th year of Henry VIII. the course was entirely altered. With a preamble stating the entire and perfect rights of the Crown of England, it gave to the Welsh all the rights and privileges of English subjects. . . . But that a nation should have a right to English liberties, and yet no share at all in the fundamental security of those liberties—the grant of their own property—seemed a thing so incongruous that, eight years after, a complete and not ill-proportioned representation by counties and boroughs was bestowed upon all Wales by Act of Parliament. From that moment, as by a charm, the tumult subsided ; obedience was restored ; peace, order, and civilisation followed in the train of liberty.

This, it must be admitted, is a rather highly-coloured representation. Thus far, at any rate, it is true that from that time to this the Welsh people have been unswervingly loyal to the English Government. During the civil wars they, for the most part, passionately espoused the cause of the King. For the last hundred or hundred and fifty years there is probably no part of the United Kingdom that has given the authorities so little trouble or anxiety. Anything like sedition, tumult, or riot is very rare in the Principality. There have been only two considerable exceptions to this rule, and these are more apparent than real. The first was the Chartist outbreak in Newport in 1839. But this was almost entirely of English inspiration, and spread over only one corner of Wales, that occupied by the mixed and half-Anglicised population of Monmouthshire and the other adjacent coal and iron districts. The great bulk of the Welsh people had no

G

share whatever in the movement, but looked upon it
with undisguised repugnance and horror. The Rebecca
disturbances of 1843 undoubtedly differed widely in this
respect, that they broke out in the very heart of the
purely Welsh population. But the character of these
also has, I believe, been greatly misunderstood in England. They had no political significance whatever, and
implied no disaffection to the Government. They
were merely uprisings, to which men were driven, or
imagined themselves driven, by the pressure of a grievance that had become intolerable, and against which
they had long in vain protested and appealed. The
thing came to pass on this wise. The small farmers of
Cardiganshire and Carmarthenshire were accustomed to
use a great deal of lime as manure. As there were no
railroads in those days, they had to send their carts for
the article to the lime-kilns, a distance of twenty, thirty,
and even forty miles. But so ingeniously had the local
magnates who had the administration of the turnpike
trusts in their hands, contrived by the multiplication of
turnpike-gates at every few miles interval along the whole
line they had to traverse, to erect obstacles in the way of
these efforts of their own tenants to improve the land
that, as the farmers have told me themselves, the prices
which they paid for the load of lime at the mouth of the
kiln, was sometimes more than doubled by the time they
got it home by these ever recurring highway imposts. At
length some of the younger men, partly in resentment
and partly in frolic, determined to take the matter into
their own hands. Forming themselves into companies,
under the guidance of a mythical female leader called
Rebecca, they sallied forth at night, pulled down the
obnoxious gates, and threw the broken timber into the
nearest river. That was the whole origin and meaning of what has been called the Rebecca Riots. No

doubt, as the thing went on, there were symptoms that a few evil-minded persons were disposed to turn the agitation to account for other and more serious purposes.

But the normal condition of the Principality is one of profound calm, rarely ruffled even by a breath of popular discontent. There is no part of the country probably where the hand of authority is so little seen and so little needed. After the Rebecca disturbances, the magistrates, taking advantage of the sort of panic felt in England rather than in Wales, succeeded in getting a county police established. I will venture to say that the men in that service are the most perfect sinecurists in the kingdom. It is really almost painful to see the worthy men—and it is no fault of theirs that they have nothing to do—parading about the small towns and villages airing their canes, for that seems the favourite symbol and instrument of office, looking in vain for some small job wherewith to relieve the *tedium vitæ*. But nothing comes in their way for months together, not even an *émeute* of small boys. Except when they are perverted from the right purpose of their office to become game-watchers for the gentry, their principal use, so far as I can see, is to touch their hats to the magistrates.

Now, surely a people thus loyal, peaceable, and orderly, may be assumed to be both qualified and entitled to have a pretty free voice in the election of those who should represent them in Parliament. And what is the present state of the Parliamentary representation of Wales? If by that term we understand that those who go to the House of Commons are supposed to represent the principles, the convictions, the interests, and the aspirations of the community in whose name they sit then it must be pronounced that the representation of the Principality is in many respects utterly anomalous and unsatisfactory. Nay, indeed, as regards some parts of the country at least, it is a mere burlesque upon the very idea of representation. Let me remind the reader of. a statement I made in the third of this series of letters, that according to Table N (p. ccc.) of Mr. Horace Mann's Report on the Census of Religious Worship, the number of persons present at the most numerously attended services on the census Sunday in 1851 in Wales, was thus distributed :—

Churchmen	. .	134,940 or 21 per cent.
Nonconformists	.	490,543 or 79 per cent.

But when we come to look at the representation we find, first, that among those sent to Parliament, there is not a single Nonconformist ; secondly, that of the thirty-two members which the Principality returns, fourteen are Conservatives, some of them of the extremest class ; and thirdly, that a considerable number of such as are nominally Liberal, are so from family tradition and political convenience, far more than from any real interest in or sympathy with the popular cause. Of the Tories, three represent boroughs and eleven counties. Of the Liberals, twelve represent boroughs and six counties. I need not say that consistent Dissenters are, and must be, from the nature of their principles and the necessity of their position, Liberals in politics. And such they have always proved to be, in fact. Such, also, beyond all doubt, are the great bulk of the Welsh Dissenters in principle and conviction. But without going into general politics, no one, at any rate, will doubt that as respects those measures which immediately affect their own interests and rights they would earnestly take the Liberal side. Let us see, then, how have they been served in regard even to these by the men who represent them in Parliament. Within the last ten or twelve years there have been several questions of this nature frequently before the Legislature—such as the question of the Irish Church, the various University Reform Bills, Mr. Hadfield's Qualification for Offices Bill, the Burials Bill, Mr. Dillwyn's Endowed Schools Bill, and the Church-rates Bill. And how have the Welsh members voted on these questions, so full of interest to their Nonconformist constituents? When in 1856 Mr. Miall brought forward his motion on the Irish Church, an institution in respect to which there has been a more general and emphatic verdict of condemnation pronounced than on almost any one of the unreformed abuses of the age, out of his 121 supporters there were only two Welsh votes. When Mr. Heywood brought forward his Oxford University Reform Bill in 1854, which gave Dissenters the right to matriculate and take degrees at the University, on every one of the divisions that took place there was a majority of Welsh votes against the measure. Again, when in 1856 the Cambridge Reform Bill was before the House, and it was proposed to give Dissenters who have taken degrees a right to sit and vote in the senate of the university, how many Welsh members supported the proposal? *Only one !* And when the proposal was afterwards modified by the restriction, that none but Episcopalians should vote on Ecclesiastical questions, there were only three Welsh votes in its favour. So that it has been truly said that, so far was Wales from having helped to pass these measures, it would have been better at that time. for the course of Liberal legislation, in regard to the universities, if Wales had been without a single representative in Parliament.

But to come down to later years. It is well known
that Mr. Hadfield has repeatedly brought forward a
measure for abolishing an offensive declaration required
of town councillors and other functionaries, which even
Lord Derby admitted is "not worth the paper on which
it was written," but which, nevertheless, is maintained
by the friends of the Church merely, to use Lord
Chelmsford's words, " as a bridle upon the consciences
of her opponents." Yet in 1861 he was supported
by only four, and in 1862 by only three, and this
year by only two Welsh votes! When Sir Morton
Peto introduced a Bill giving the right to Dissenting
ministers to officiate in parochial churchyards, as
has already been done in Scotland, Ireland, and most
of our colonies, there were eight Welsh votes in its
favour, and twelve against it. It fared somewhat
better with Mr. Dillwyn's Endowed Schools Bill, which
in 1861 was supported by ten Welsh members, and
opposed by nine.

As respects Church-rates, eight years ago only twelve
Welsh members voted for their abolition. But on this
question there has been a gradual and progressive improvement, since, on the last division, that which has
lately taken place, there were sixteen for and only six
against it. But the marvel is, that with the immense
majority of the population holding such views as they do,
any of the members for Wales should vote for the old
ideas of ecclesiastical exclusiveness and ascendancy. In
order to bring into bolder relief the flagrant anomalies of
Welsh representation in this respect, let me ask the
reader's attention to the following tabular statement, in
which he will find presented in detail the general result
already given as to the proportionate numbers of worshippers in Churches and Dissenting chapels on the
census Sunday:—

Counties.	Number of attendants at the most numerously attended Service on the Census Sunday.	
	Church.	Nonconformist.
Anglesea	2,374	16,604
Brecknock . . . , .	6,234	19,375
Cardigan	10,517	34,571
Carmarthen	8,685	31,918
Carnarvon	7,328	41,781
Denbigh	9,138	29,153
Flint	4,931	13,046
Glamorgan	11,997	81,141
Merioneth	2,360	20,168
Monmouth	16,026	48,201
Montgomery	8,370	22,441
Pembroke.	8,989	21,839
Radnor	4,259	3,958

Here it will be seen that in every one of the Welsh counties, except Radnorshire, not only do the Dissenters preponderate, but they do so in so enormous a degree as to make the comparison almost ridiculous. And yet eleven out of the seventeen men representing these counties are Tories. Take, as an illustration, two examples, one from North and one from South Wales. In Carnarvonshire the Churchmen are to Dissenters as 7,328 to 41,781; in Carmarthenshire they are as 8,685 to 31,918. And yet Colonel Pennant and Mr. David Jones vote doggedly against every measure introduced into Parliament for the relief of Dissenters. They vote in favour of imposing for ever upon the immense majority of their constituents an impost for supporting the churches of the minority, although they must know that the former maintain, at their own proper cost, scores, if not hundreds, of places of worship from which, as they must also perfectly well know, flow the influences that have done so much to enlighten, and civilise, and refine the people. They vote for excluding the children of three-fourths of those whom they profess to represent from all share in the education given at the national universities. They vote against giving even so small a relief to the consciences of their Nonconformist constituents as is involved in abolishing a declaration which, it is openly admitted, has no value whatever except as a means of humiliating and affronting them. They vote against granting permission to bereaved and mourning families, while their wounds are yet green from the stroke of death, to have the satisfaction of listening to a few words of consolation and prayer over the grave of the beloved from the lips of their own ministers. They vote in support of perpetuating a monopoly as respects endowed grammar schools, the effect of which is, among other things, to brand every individual among the tens of thousands of Dissenters whom they pretend to represent as a person who cannot be deemed in law an "honest and discreet man." Said I not well, then, when I declared that the representation of some parts of Wales is a mere burlesque upon the name of representation? Take, again, the case of Denbighshire, where Churchmen are to Dissenters as 9,130 to 29,153; and yet the gentleman who nominally represents this county is a Tory of the "straitest sect." He and his family have pertinaciously opposed every one of the great reforms that have taken place in this country for the last forty years. And ever since he has been in Parliament he has resisted even the smallest concession to the claims and the feelings of the class who constitute the overwhelming majority of the people in whose name he professes to sit in that assembly. I ask again, is not this a mere burlesque of representation? Sir Watkin Williams Wynn may represent the broad acres of which, by the accident of birth, he is the fortunate possessor; but that he represents the *people* of Denbighshire, their real convictions, interests, desires, and aims, it would be simply preposterous to believe.

I may be asked, If this be the state of things as respects the representation of the Principality, why is it so? Why do not the people send other and different men to Parliament? These are the questions which I shall try to the best of my ability to answer in my next letters.

LETTER XI.

CAUSES OF THE ANOMALIES IN POLITICAL REPRESENTA-TION—SLOW GROWTH OF INTEREST IN POLITICS.

In my last letter I [anticipated that, in connection with the view I had given of the Parliamentary representation of the Principality as anomalous and unsatisfactory, questions like these might occur to the reader:—Why does such a state of things prevail? If Dissenters out-number Churchmen in the proportion stated, how comes it to pass that the representation of the country should be exclusively in the hands of Churchmen, many of them persons of the very narrowest views on all political and ecclesiastical questions? These are inquiries which I shall now endeavour to answer.

And, in the first place, it must be confessed, that it is only within a comparatively late period that the Welsh people have begun to take an intelligent and earnest in-terest in politics. Not but that the Principality before that was sometimes as violently agitated as other parts of the country by electioneering excitements ; but usually the conflict turned much more upon persons than princi-ples. Certain great families, who by tradition or accident, rather than from conviction, had come to espouse one side or the other in politics, held it a matter of hereditary honour to contest the representation with each other, far

less as a means of giving effect to any particular views of
State policy, than of asserting and maintaining their own
family consequence against rival claimants in a county or
neighbourhood. In times preceding the religious revival
of last century the bulk of the people were content to
leave the question of political principle, if indeed any
such were involved, in the hands of these local magnates,
enlisting under the banners they unfurled with unquestioning faith and devotion. Whatever of enthusiasm,
therefore, they felt in electioneering struggles was less
that of citizens contending for their rights than of clansmen vehemently battling for their respective chieftains.
But the movement to which I have referred laid the foundation for a change in all this, the operation of which,
though not immediate and obvious, was ultimately sure
and inevitable. You cannot vivify a nation's life with
new and earnest religious convictions without influencing
its character in other directions than those which are expressly religious. When the light which Christianity
sheds upon our spiritual nature and relations dawns upon
the mind of a man, however profound may be the abase-
ment which, on the one hand, it may lead him to feel, as
in the presence of the Supreme, it cannot fail, on the
other, to awaken within him some perceptions of the
essential and indestructible dignity and worth of the individual human soul, as illustrated by facts of awful and
mysterious import, in comparison with which the conventional distinctions of rank and wealth that prevail in
society pale into utter insignificance. He who in the
light of those facts has learnt to fear God is less likely
thenceforward to be stricken with any servile or paralysing
fear of man, even though that man were a squire or a
landlord. Besides which it is not in the nature of things
that those who have been driven to assert their independence in matters of religion should long continue to

be slaves in matters of politics. And the same law acts, though more slowly, on the character of communities as of individuals. The whole history of the past proves that, at a longer or shorter interval, the one result invariably follows the other. Nowhere has this fact received a more signal illustration than in our own national history. Who does not know that the political struggle which secured the liberties of Englishmen was largely the effect of the new spiritual life which the Reformation had infused into the heart of the nation ? And so, according to the judgment of a most competent witness, has it been everywhere else. " Almost every effort," says De Tocqueville, " made by the moderns towards liberty has been occasioned by the desire to manifest or to defend their religious convictions."

Such, also, has been the result of the renewal of religious life in the Principality of Wales, though certain causes have been at work there which have considerably retarded its natural development. During the actual period of the revival itself the national mind and heart were pre-occupied with that, and the responsibilities and duties which sprung out of it. That time, when they were passing from death to life, was a very solemn time with the Welsh people ; a time of intense and absorbing emotion, which left them little leisure or thought for secular politics. It was not possible at such a moment to combine the two things in their regard, and since it was necessary to choose between the two, no one can question that they chose wisely. Spiritual life first, and political rights and privileges afterwards. I, for one, cannot, therefore, profess to grudge the time lost by the Welsh people as respects political action, when I know how that time was employed, in carrying light into the dark parts of the country, in gathering churches, building chapels, establishing and organising Sunday-schools, and

extending and perfecting that apparatus of evangelical
agency which has been of such incalculable service to
the moral and religious life of the nation.

And even after the first stress of this work was over,
many of the leaders of that movement had a strong repugnance to see their disciples mixing in the strife of
politics, and that from a feeling for which it is impossible
not to cherish a large measure of respect. Having, with
infinite labour and travail of soul, rescued many of these
novices from a state of the lowest ignorance and degra-
dation, they were apprehensive, and not without reason,
that if drawn, while their religious character was yet
immature, into the vortex of electioneering excitement—
as elections are unhappily too often conducted—they
might fall back into the evil habits from which they had
been with so much difficulty reclaimed. But there was
another sentiment far less defensible at the bottom of
the antipathy which some of these good men felt for
politics, traces of which may be still found lingering in
many minds. They seemed to consider politics themselves as something common and unclean, unworthy the
regard of those who aspired to a saintly profession. It
is difficult to know how such a feeling could have
originated among men who theologically were very much
the heirs of the Puritans. But however it originated, it
cannot be too strongly repudiated, as utterly false in
principle, and of most disastrous practical consequence.
Very admirable seem to me the remarks of De Tocqueville on the subject. Speaking of ministers of religion
he says :—

I do not ask them to make those whom they educate or influence
Republicans or Royalists ; but I wish they would more frequently
tell them that, while Christians, they also belong to one of the
great human societies which God has formed, apparently in order
to show more clearly the ties by which individuals ought to be
mutually attached—societies which are called nations, inhabiting

a territory which they call their country. I wish them to instil
into their very souls, that every one belongs much more to this
collective Being than he does to himself, that towards this Being
no one ought to be indifferent, much less, by treating such indifference as a sort of languid virtue, to enervate many of our
noblest instincts ; that everyone is responsible for the fortunes of
this collective Being ; that everyone is bound to work out its
prosperity, and to watch that it be not governed except by
respectable, beneficent, and legitimate authorities. . . . Without doubt Christianity can exist under every Government. This
is an evidence of its truth. It never has been bound, and never
will be bound, to any form of government, or to the grandeur of
any single nation. It can reign in the worst Governments, and
extracts from the calamities which they inflict the occasion for
admirable virtues ; but it does not follow that it ought to render us
insensible or even indifferent to those calamities, or that it does not
impose on every citizen the duty of boldly striving to abate them
by all the means which his conscience indicates and approves.

Well, owing to the operation of the various causes I
have indicated, there came upon Wales a season of great
political apathy. It was a period of transition. The
time for the politics of blind partisanship was gone. The
time for the politics of intelligent conviction had not yet
come. One formidable obstacle in the way of this was
the difference of language, which cut the people off from
the political literature of England. At first, their own
periodical literature, being, like almost everything else
that was good among them, the offspring of the religious
revival, took its character from the cause whence it had
arisen. It was almost exclusively religious. I remember
when I was a boy that all the politics of the magazine
received in my father's house were compressed into about
half a page of most insipid summary at the end. It
is scarcely more than twenty years since the Welsh
began to have anything like a political literature. Much,
indeed, had been done before that, through the medium
of the monthly periodicals, to awaken something like a
public spirit in the nation. There were two men
especially who deserve most honourable mention in
connection with this department of service, namely, the

Rev. Joseph Harris, of Swansea, and the Rev. David
Rees, of Llanelly. As editors of two of the principal
monthly serials, which they conducted with eminent
ability and earnestness, they did much to stimulate
popular intelligence on other than mere religious questions, and to prepare men for taking up the active duties
of citizenship.

The Welsh newspaper press has a history of its own
not without interest and instruction. The first newspaper in the Welsh language that was successfully
established began to be published at Liverpool in the
year 1843, under the name of *Yr Amserau*, or *The Times;*
for though several attempts of a similar nature had been
previously made, they had uniformly failed. This paper
appeared at first fortnightly, and afterwards weekly,
and owes its success almost entirely to the patriotic
and disinterested devotion of one man—the Rev.
William Rees, of Liverpool, now Dr. Rees,* of Chester,
a gentleman of high character, rare abilities, and in-
vincible energy, all of which he ungrudgingly dedicated, without fee or reward, to the service of his
countrymen. For nearly ten years Mr. Rees bore the
whole burden of editorship; and to edit a Welsh weekly
paper is a very different thing from editing an English
weekly. In the former case there can be none of the
paste and scissors work in which the latter saves so large
a portion of labour. Owing to the difference of language,
every scrap of general intelligence, foreign news, extracts
from Parliamentary debates, reports of English public
meetings, records of remarkable events, etc., have to pass
through the editor's pen, by being either translated or
re-written. Most of this enormous labour Mr. Rees
underwent, in addition to furnishing all the leading

* While this book is passing through the press, this admirable
and distinguished man has departed from us, full of years and
honours, amid the universal lamentations of the people whom
he so long and so well served.

articles and other original contributions, which were
written with admirable intelligence and vigour, assisted
in some of the minor duties of editorship, and that for
only a portion of the time, by the successive publishers
of the paper, Mr. Jones and Mr. Lloyd, who also made
no small sacrifices, personal and pecuniary, in sustaining
the enterprise. I feel pleasure in paying my tribute of
admiration and respect to these men, to whom, and emphatically to Mr. Rees, the Welsh people owe so much
in connection with their political literature. It may be
readily imagined that the odious imposts, justly called
"taxes on knowledge," in the form of stamp, advertise-
ment, and paper duty, which, at that time, so fettered
the action of the press, weighed cruelly upon a paper
struggling with so many peculiar difficulties. To escape
from a part of this pressure, the publisher at one time
took the paper to be printed at Douglas, in the Isle of
Man, that island being exempt from some of those exac-
tions. And then occurred an incident which I record
with indignation and shame. Might it not have been
expected that the professed leaders of the people, the
gentry and clergy of Wales, would have sympathised
with the efforts of the brave men who, at such sacrifice
of time, labour and money, were thus endeavouring to
promote the political instruction of their countrymen?
Instead of which, what did they do? Why, the gentry
and clergy of North Wales held a meeting in the city
of Bangor, and adopted a memorial to the Government, calling attention to the fact that this solitary,
struggling Welsh newspaper—mentioning it by name—
was being published in the Isle of Man, and sug-
gesting that it was not lawful to take a British
paper to be published there. Surely it is not easy to
conceive of anything more utterly mean, paltry, and
despicable, than this act of the parsons and landowners
of the country assembling in solemn conclave to use their

combined influence to try to extinguish, by means of a
legal technicality, the only publication through which
their countrymen could at that time receive any regular
supply of political intelligence, merely because it advo-
cated opinions different from theirs. It was, nevertheless, an act rich in significance. Those associated in it
paid unwittingly the highest compliment they could have
paid to Mr. Rees and his coadjutors. By a sagacious
though selfish instinct, they felt with unerring certainty
that the light which was being let in on the minds of the
people could not fail to prove damaging to their pretensions and practices. That light, therefore, must, if possible, be shut out at any expense, even at the expense of
obliging the collective chivalry and spirituality of the
Tory party in North Wales to stoop to so shabby a pro-
ceeding as the one I have described. Happily for them,
there was a Conservative Government in power at the
time, who responded without delay to the generous
appeal, declared that the publication of a Welsh newspaper in the Isle of Man was illegal, and must be desisted
from forthwith. The promoters of the memorial were
jubilant at the success of their intrigue, thinking that
they had now beyond doubt crushed the obnoxious sheet.
I am happy to say they were mistaken. The paper
survived their onslaught, and lived to grow what it is at
the present moment, a thriving and prosperous concern,
the father of a long line of such, for there are now at
least eight newspapers published in the Welsh language.
But this little episode is one which the people of Wales
will do well not speedily to forget.

It will thus be seen that if the Nonconformists of the
Principality have not yet contributed so large a share of
influence in support of the Liberal cause as, from their
numbers and intelligence, we had a right to expect, much
may be said to explain and extenuate the default. They

had much other and most momentous work to do. Their political education had only recently began, and is yet comparatively imperfect. Still, great progress has been made. The schoolmaster is unmistakably abroad. The leaven of independent thought is spreading rapidly through society, and if my countrymen will only display in vindication of their political freedom one half the firmness in encountering persecutions and enduring sacrifices which their fathers did in vindication of their religious freedom, the day of their emancipation is not far distant. How real and how severe those persecutions and sacrifices still are it will be my business to show in my next letter.

LETTER XII.

CAUSES OF ANOMALIES IN THE POLITICAL REPRESENTA-
TION—INFLUENCE OF THE CLERGY.

I REMARKED in my last letter that the comparative political apathy into which, for reasons I attempted to explain, the Welsh people had fallen during the last three-quarters of a century or more, had for several years past been gradually disappearing. In the Principality, as elsewhere, the cheap newspaper press has been doing its work. It is not in vain that so much stirring intelligence and discussion have percolated through the public mind. I might refer to many pregnant indications of the awakening of political life among my countrymen. Even so far back as 1842 there was a conference of Welsh ministers, principally of the independent and Baptist denominations, held at Carnarvon, to promote the abolition of the Corn Laws. Mr. Prentice, the historian of the League, says of that

H

meeting "that the proceedings were distinguished throughout by talent, fervour, and unanimity." Four or five years ago there was a more general conference held at Swansea, when a standing committee was appointed to watch over the political interests of the Dissenting community in South Wales. Some incidents connected with the last. election, also, were full of significance as to the change which is, by degrees, being wrought in the popular feeling on this subject. But in proportion as these signs of activity and independence multiply, will the efforts to quash them be redoubled, on the part of those classes who seem to imagine that they have by prescription the right to possess a monopoly of political power. Past experience proves that they are ready to have recourse to very unscrupulous means to accomplish their object. As I have previously intimated, the people must stand prepared to make great sacrifices if they would have their Parliamentary representation a reality and not a pretence. If I am asked what kind of sacrifice, I answer every kind of sacrifice involved in resisting those influences and measures put in force to suppress or to punish the free expression of political opinion, with which we are familiar enough in England, but which are employed in Wales in more severe and summary forms, and with a more open and daring defiance of justice and decency. The ruin of tradesmen by withdrawal of custom; the expulsion of some tenants from their holdings; the exaction from others of increased and extortionate rents; the worrying out of the lives of others by long-suspended threats of some terrible retribution that is coming upon them; the withholding from religious bodies of sites on which to build schools and places of worship; and, in some instances, the actual confiscation and sale of chapels built with public money—these, and such as these, are the practices to which Welsh landlords do not scruple to have recourse, in order to coerce the consciences of their neighbours.

But, before furnishing some illustrations of these state-ments, let me try to explain how the population of Wales is divided as regards politics. I am confident that no one competently acquainted with the country will deny that a large numerical majority of the constituents are Liberals of a very decided character. For in Wales, as in this country, it is not the Dissenters merely that are Liberal, but a considerable proportion also of the members of the Church of England. And, if there were perfect freedom of voting, I doubt if a single Tory would be returned for any part of the Principality. But there are certain classes who, from position, concert, and audacity, have hitherto contrived to impose the opinions of the minority upon not a few of the Welsh constituencies.

These classes are mainly three—first, the clergy; secondly, the gentry ; and, thirdly, a class of agents, or stewards, generally of the legal profession, who act as a sort of middlemen between the gentry and the people. And, first, as to the clergy. I have no wish to say any-teing disrespectful or unkind of the ministers of the Establishment in the Principality. There are among them men of piety, learning, and eloquence, who would do honour to any church. From their body also have come some most valuable contributions to the works serving to illustrate the language and literature of their country. The names of the Rev. Edward Davies, author of " The Celtic Researches," and " The Myth-ology of the British Druids ;" the Rev. Evan Evans, author of " Dissertatio de Bardis ;" the Rev. Thomas Price, the historian of Wales ; the Rev. D. Sylvan Evans, who shares with Dr. Owen Pugh the honour of

H 2

being its lexicographer, and others I could mention, can never be repeated without respect and gratitude by every Welsh scholar and patriot. The Welsh clergy, moreover, are entitled to the credit—no small one, surely, in these days—of having kept to the *via media* of a sober, Evangelical Christianity, without rushing to either extreme of Puseyism or Colensoism, between which the teaching of their Church seems now oscillating like a pendulum. Of late years, indeed, I believe that a very small number of them have somewhat inclined in the former direction, so far, at least, as to repeat some of the inexpressibly silly twaddle in which none but the silliest of the High Church party in England think it wise to indulge against Dissenters, by representing them as followers of Korah, Dathan, Abiram, whom the earth, I suppose, if it were at all properly alive to its duty, and not so perversely schismatical in its sympathies, ought long ere this to have swallowed up alive. It is only fair, however, to say that the most violent specimens of this class in Wales are renegade Dissenters, who are trying, apparently, to purge themselves of the taint of ancient schism still hanging round them, and to curry favour with those who probably look upon their accession as a very equivocal honour, by vulgar and violent abuse of their former associates. But as is generally the case with men of that order, they only succeed in being as cordially despised by those whom they have joined, as by those whom they have left. I am far from including in this description all the modern conformists. Among them, as among the general body of the clergy, there are catholic-minded and kind-hearted gentlemen, who live on pleasant terms with their Dissenting neighbours, and do not disdain sometimes to join in their religious services. And if there be a much larger number of a different spirit, that is owing, no doubt, in a

great measure, to the fact, that as the ministers of a
Church imposed by the State, but repudiated by the
people, they are placed in an utterly false, and I should
think most painful, position. Indeed, I hardly know of
any class—I say it not sarcastically but quite sincerely—
more to be pitied than are many of the Welsh clergy.
While hypothetically—according to the *theory* of the
parochial system—they are the spiritual teachers and
leaders of the whole parish, practically they find their
ministerial and pastoral guidance renounced by a large
majority of the people, who look upon them, I fear, with
feelings the reverse of reverence, as men who are receiving hire for labour, the greater part of which is done by
others. Or, where high personal character triumphs
over this kind of prejudice, "it is a very common remark," as Mr. Johnes says in his " Essay on the Causes
of Dissent," " that when the clergyman is beloved it is
rather as a benevolent layman than as a clergyman, and
that even then the people chiefly confide in the Dissenting ministers for guidance and consolation." They are
thus cut off from that pleasant fellowship in intercourse
and effort with the mass of their parishioners in which a
a good clergyman finds his congenial sphere of activity
and enjoyment. As they are for the most part men of
the people, the gentry, though attending their churches,
and accessible to their influence, do not very much court
their society, or if they do, it is in a patronising and half-
contemptuous spirit, which, as high-minded men, they
cannot but feel and resent. Thus isolated to a great
extent in their own parishes, they are driven very much
to consort with each other, so that their minds, as it
were, breed inwards, a process not favourable to liberal
thought and generous feeling. While compelled to bear
so anomalous a character—pastors without a flock—seeing the chapels crowded with fervid worshippers and

active workers, while their own churches are comparatively deserted and lifeless, it is not in human nature but that they should feel bitterly mortified, a feeling which some of the weakest among them poorly attempt to disguise by assuming towards Dissenters in general, and towards Dissenting ministers in particular, an air of great *hauteur* and superiority, which, under the circumstances, is sufficiently ludicrous. But when the time of election comes they are avenged. I hardly need say that, with exceptions as rare as black swans, they are, politically, Tories of the rankest description. Their own direct influence is often very inconsiderable, except in the rare cases where they are landowners as well as clergymen. But their influence indirectly is very great. Scattered as they are all over the country, and living among the people, though apart from them, they form collectively a sort of huge Dionysius' ear for their party, to gather and convey to the landlords every whisper of disaffection against the political despotism which the latter are disposed to exercise over their tenants and dependents. It is to be feared, also, that such reports lose nothing in rancour by thus filtrating through minds soured by sectarian and professional jealousy. And when the actual time of conflict comes, it is, of course, an immense advantage to a Conservative candidate to have in every parish an amateur electioneering agent, who is spurred to vigilance and activity quite as much by personal feeling as by public principle, and finds, perhaps, a not ungrateful compensation for years of humiliation and neglect by seeing the Dissenting schismatics who forsake his guidance and slight his eloquence in favour of the conventicle, writhing under the harrow of an arrogant and tyrannical landlordism. And the general belief is— I sincerely hope that in this respect they are wronged— that when any of the people dare to assert their own

manhood by voting in harmony with their political convictions, and against the wishes of their landlords, *they*
are the foremost to counsel and instigate severe measures
of retribution against the recalcitrants.

No one has a right to doubt the perfect sincerity with
which the Welsh clergy take their side in politics. Nay,
indeed, it must be admitted that in resisting all Liberal
measures—in defending all ancient abuses—in setting
themselves to oppose, tooth and nail, every step in the
direction of freedom, whether civil, religious, commercial,
or literary—they are only abiding faithful to the traditions of their Church. Such, if we may trust the
testimony of two great writers, both of them, I believe,
members of her communion, has been the policy of that
Church from its foundation. But the word "Church" in
this case can certainly only apply to the clergy, as it
would be most ungrateful to forget that among the lay
members of the Church of England there always have
been and still are as genuine and dauntless friends of
freedom as among any religious body whatever. But,
with this qualification, I am afraid, the words of the
writers to whom I have referred cannot be impeached.
"The Church of England," says Lord Macaulay, "has
continued to be for more than one hundred and fifty
years the steady enemy of public liberty. The divine
right of. kings and the duty of passively obeying all their
commands were her favourite tenets. She held these
tenets firmly through times of oppression, persecution,
and licentiousness—while law was trampled down, while
judgment was perverted, while the people were eaten as
though they were bread. Once, and but once—for a
moment, and but for a moment—when her own dignity
and property were touched she forgot to practise the
submission she had taught." No less emphatic is
the language of Mr. Lecky in his great work on "The

Progress of Rationalism." " No other Church," he says,
" has so uniformly betrayed and trampled on the liberties
of her country. In all those fiery trials through which
English liberty has passed since the Reformation she
invariably cast her influence into the scale of tyranny,
supported and eulogised every attempt to violate the
Constitution, and wrote the fearful sentence of eternal
condemnation   upon   the   tombs   of   the   martyrs of
freedom."*

I am bound, therefore, to vindicate the perfect con-
sistency of my clerical compatriots in espousing that
party in politics which resists all progress and reform.
But however strictly they may continue in the line of
political orthodoxy according to the tenets of their
Church, it is none the less true that they are in direct
antagonism to the convictions and wishes of the great
bulk of their countrymen.   And surely the reflection
must sometimes force itself upon the more thoughtful of
them, that it is a most unhappy relation to exist between
any body of Christian ministers and the people among
whom they dwell, when they are regarded, not as friends
and counsellors sympathising with their views and aiding
in the attainment of their objects, but as spies and
informers, who watch their proceedings only to betray
them, who are always strenuously opposed to them or
all public questions, conspiring for their defeat, exulting
in their humiliation, and lending themselves as willing
accomplices, if not instruments, in the oppressions practised upon them for the free exercise of their political
rights.   Is it thus they hope to command the respect
and win back the alienated affections of their flocks?
When an established Church has so lost the confidence
of the inhabitants of a country that it comes to be looked
upon, not as a sanctuary for rest or refuge, but as a

* Vol. II., p. 193.

hostile garrison from which the population receives only provocation and annoyance, instead of protection and succour, it will be impossible long to prevent awkward questions arising in many minds as to how far, even on mere principles of political expediency, it is consonant with justice and reason to perpetuate such an institution.

LETTER XIII.

POLITICAL INFLUENCE OF THE GENTRY.

IN my last letter I explained the position which the clergy occupy in Wales, and the influence they exercise in political affairs. I pass on now to the gentry. The great majority of this class are Tories of the purest water, who have clung through evil report and through good report to the dismal creed which makes the safety of society depend upon putting the utmost restriction upon every form of liberty, whether liberty of speech, or conscience, or worship, or trade, or voting. There are a few great houses who have always championed the Liberal cause as a sort of family heirloom. But there have been some ugly indications of late that, whatever may have been the case with their ancestors, the present race would far sooner sacrifice their professed political principles than see any part of the representation of the country passing out of the hands of their own class.

There is, thus, I fear, a wide separation in conviction and sympathy between the great bulk of the people and those who assume to be their leaders. I cannot honestly say that I consider the blame to rest with the former. Lack of loyalty is not the failing of any branch of the

Celtic race. Indeed, an exaggerated tendency in the opposite direction, expressing itself by a too enthusiastic and indiscriminate devotion to their chief, is regarded by many as the sin which doth most easily beset them. Nay, some philosophical historians, who love to indulge in large generalisations, have professed to find in this, the characteristic distinction between the Celt and the Teuton, that the former loves the rule of persons and the latter of institutions. Be that as it may, it is very certain that there was no indisposition on the part of the Welsh people to trust and to follow as their natural leaders those, at least, of the gentry who are, or who profess to be, the descendants of their own ancient princes. It is one of the current delusions which prevail in England about Wales, which had its origin, no doubt, in what was at one time something like a reality, that there are certain great families in the Principality whom all Welshmen regard with an almost servile and superstitious veneration. That may have been the case formerly, though not to the absurd excess which our English friends imagine, and it might have been the case still had those great families taken the smallest pains to cultivate or even to retain the confidence and affection of the people, by keeping themselves in any degree within the sphere of their sympathies. But they have not done this. They have done the very reverse of this. They have acted in reference to matters which their countrymen have come to regard as dearer to them than their heart's blood, as if they wished and intended to alienate their hearts from them. I can bear witness to the fact—for there is a great difference in this respect even since the days of my childhood—that my countrymen did, with a very touching fidelity, try hard and long to believe in their old ancestral gentry, and it is not their fault, I repeat, if the spell of allegiance is now almost completely broken. You cannot, with the best intentions, long venerate what is not venerable.

I am far from wishing to include all the class in the same condemnation. Among the Welsh gentry there are some most estimable gentlemen, affable neighbours, kind landlords, large-hearted and liberal-minded men, who, though Churchmen themselves, are not only fair but generous in their treatment of Dissenters. As landlords they are perhaps more careless than might be desired, content with a very slovenly cultivation of their lands and not much given to encourage improvements. But they are forbearing and indulgent to their tenants, exacting very moderate rents, letting their farms remain in occupation of the same families for generations, when, no doubt, they might obtain from others higher rents, and a more enterprising tillage. And these are rewarded by the respect and attachment of the whole community, which they may long retain if they are wise enough not to strain those feelings by attempting to exercise a coercive influence in matters that lie quite beyond the relations between landlords and tenants.

But there is another section whose conduct even as landlords shows that there exists almost as urgent a necessity for a Tenant Right law for some parts of Wales as for Ireland. There lies before me now a pamphlet, published some ten years ago, called " Diosg Farm: a Sketch of its History." It was written by a man known and honoured throughout the Principality, whose veracity is beyond impeachment or suspicion. It narrates the story of the occupation, first by his father and then by his widowed mother, of the above farm on the estate of one of the greatest landowners in North Wales. The substance of it may be stated in a few sentences. John Roberts was an Independent minister, labouring among a poor and scattered population, in a remote mountain district of Merionethshire. To eke out the scanty pittance with which alone the poor mountaineers could reward his pious labours, he kept a school, by which he did an inestimable service to the cause of education in the district. He was a man of singular excellence of character, peaceful, and a peacemaker, gentle, unworldly, and long-suffering almost to a fault. After he had been settled about ten years in the above neighbourhood, Diosg Farm became vacant. " It was a wet, cold, stony, bramble-bush, north-aspect farm on the sunless side of a very steep hill. It was then in a much worse condition than it could have been in any wilderness state. The old rush-thatched house and barn were in rotten ruins." It remained long unoccupied. No one dared touch so bank-rupt and hopeless a concern. Least of all did it enter the mind of John Roberts to meddle with it. But an overture was made to him by the representatives of the landlord urging him to take the farm, with the assurance that if he would consent to undergo some privations and make some sacrifices for a few years, the kind-hearted, noble-minded lord of that farm would be " sure to let him have compound interest for his labour and capital." Seduced by these promises, in an evil hour, and, after long hesitation, he took the farm. John Roberts was one of those men who carried his conscience into every- thing, even into the cultivation of the soil. He did so in this case. He entered upon the work of reclaiming this miserable holding with a quiet energy and persever-ance that were characteristic of the man. He drained, and sub-soiled, and manured, made roads and fences, and helped largely by money and labour to rebuild the house and out-buildings. And then, after he had been engaged on this work for not quite seven years, having expended £700, the savings of his whole life, and the

modest dowry of his wife, and while he was so imper-
fectly even beginning to reap the reward of his toils, that
he was still obliged to buy bread for his farm servants,
then the very men, stewards of this great landed proprietor, who had tempted him to take the farm, and
cheered him on in the laborious and costly improvements
he was making, by repeated promises of a liberal compensation hereafter, suddenly brought a land-surveyor on
the farm, who, without making any inquiry whatever as
to what John Roberts had done, advanced his rent at
once full fifty per cent.   He appealed against this
decision, pointed out how much he had invested in the
land, but the only answer to his remonstrances was a
peremptory declaration that if he did not choose to pay
the advanced rent the farm would be let for the same
rent to another ; that is to say, the new comer was to
have it for the same rent as was demanded of the man
whose £700 was fast buried in its drains and roads, and
fences and buildings.   This, I am afraid, is only a specimen of what often takes place, the only difference being
that in this case the son of John Roberts, being a man
of education and spirit, and wielding a very incisive pen,
has been able to drag the matter into light.

The mania for game-preserving is also carried to a
most absurd and ruinous extent on some estates in Wales.
The land swarms with wild animals, who feed on the
farmer's crops, and are kept by the landlord not for sport
but profit, regular supplies being sent weekly to the
market at Liverpool or elsewhere, while the unfortunate
cultivator of the soil has no right to claim any compensation for the havoc committed on his property.   Such
things as these, it will be readily imagined, do not breed
love and reverence towards the owners of the soil.

Other circumstances also serve to widen the chasm
between the gentry and the people.   Many of the former

are ignorant of the language of the country, and are rather proud of their ignorance, while others, who have acquired a little smattering of colloquial Welsh, make no attempt to acquaint themselves with the current periodical literature, through which, in Wales as everywhere else, the national mind and heart and will find expression. This is not a sentimental, but a very real and serious grievance ; for the people among whom] they dwell remain unknown to the upper classes, or rather, what is far worse, they are misknown, the impressions of them which they receive being conveyed through a false medium —the medium of minds coloured and distorted by interest or prejudice. To the same influence I suppose we must ascribe the fact that many of them tease and worry the people by petty persecutions about their chapels and schools. Some landlords positively refuse to grant sites on any terms on which Dissenters can build schoolrooms and places of worship. I have several recent cases of that kind mentioned in a letter now before me, in which the names of all the parties concerned are given very explicitly, with full liberty to publish them on the authority of the writer. But as I wish to avoid all appearance of personality I shall not reveal the names unless I am challenged to do so. Other landlords, while reluctantly and most ungraciously granting a site, after sometimes keeping ministers and congregations dancing attendance upon them, cap in hand, it may be for months or even years, will on no consideration give them even a lease ; and thus they oblige the people either to go without the means of worshipping God according to their consciences, or to put down buildings costing many hundreds of pounds, on the land of men whom they know to be hostile or prejudiced, without any security whatever but the honour or caprice of the proprietor. And when the time of election comes advantage is occasionally taken of this in the meanest spirit, by holding threats over the heads of congregations, threats which, in some instances, have been actually carried into effect, of ejecting them from their chapels or of selling the building over their heads.

This kind of petty sectarian spite which refuses sites for building Dissenting chapels and schools is familiarly enough known in England. But there are two things which serve greatly to aggravate the hardship in Wales. The first is, that it is not a small minority, but the great bulk of the population, who are Dissenters, for whom, even if they were disposed to go to the parish church, there would in many cases be no accommodation, and in some no instruction in the only language they can understand. The second is, that, as the estates of these gentlemen bigots often extend over a whole county, there is no chance for the poor people of finding any other spot on which to put down the ark of the covenant of their God.

Surely every one must feel that all this is a cruel and tyrannous abuse of the rights of property, which, if perseveringly and extensively practised, may give rise to questions the discussion of which it will be best not to provoke. When the Free Church secession took place in Scotland, some of the great Scotch landlords showed a disposition to try to crush that young and vigorous community by having recourse to similar tactics. They drove the people assembling to worship off their lands, and obliged them to seek refuge on board ships on the sea or on the lakes. But by degrees there came a very dangerous gleam into the eyes of the children of the Covenanters before which those territorial potentates thought it wise to recoil in time. The Welsh gentry also will find it to their own honour and comfort not to pursue that policy too far. No one wants to call in question the rights of property, but there is one other species of rights which is still more sacred, namely, the rights of conscience. What renders this course more utterly indefensible is the fact, which is known, or ought to be known, to these gentlemen, that to the Dissenting chapels and Sunday schools which they are so anxious to banish from their domains, they owe that enlightening and civilising influence on the minds and character of the people, which confers such absolute security on their own persons and possessions, and adds incalculably even to the mere pecuniary value of their estates.   There are great capabilities of crime, not of the mean, but of the violent order, in the Celtic character, as is unhappily too abundantly proved by the history of Ireland.   But, as my friend Dr. Rees, of Swansea, says, in one of his able papers, " In Wales no landowner, proprietor of works, or any other member of the upper classes, has cause to be afraid of the dagger of the assassin, the fire of the incendiary, or the rude assaults of the infuriated mob." And does it never occur to these gentlemen to inquire the reason why ? It is not always, they may be assured, from either fear or love of them.

The writer of a vigorous article, which appeared in one of the Welsh quarterlies, called Y *Traethodydd* (" The Essayist"), on certain incidents connected with the last election, has some admirable remarks on this subject. He is referring to the pretension that had been put forward by, or on behalf of, some of the candidates, that Dissenters ought implicitly to vote for them because they had granted leases on which to build chapels.

We know (says the writer), through the testimony of pious clergymen who lived in those days, what was the social, educational, and religious condition of the Principality before the appearance of Nonconformity, and we know what it is at present, after Nonconformity has been the means, among its other achievements, of reforming the Established Church itself, and bringing it to emulate its own efforts, and so to co-operate in the improvement in every respect of the population of Wales. But we unhesitatingly affirm that the landowners of Wales are under far greater obligations to the Nonconformists of Wales than the Nonconformists are to them. And while it is becoming that we should approach the owners of the soil as gentlemen, it is utterly unworthy of our ancestry and of our history that we should crouch before them like spaniels. Is it not in our sanctuaries that the people are taught to fear God and to honour their rulers, to pay honour to whom honour is due, and tribute to whom tribute, and to do good to all men, even to our enemies? Are not our Sunday School teachers the unpaid police of the Principality? Is it not the piety of the members of our churches that has saved many an oppressor from being shot from behind a hedge, as has often been done to obnoxious landlords in Ireland? It is the fear of God in the hearts of those thousands of our people, whom some graceless and ungrateful sprigs of gentility are wont to call "canting Methodists," that protects the person, the palaces, and the possessions of those who have sometimes sorely persecuted them, and treated them as if they were evildoers.

LETTER XIV.

POLITICAL LANDLORDISM IN WALES.

CAN any one explain what there is in the relation between a tenant farmer and his landlord so essentially different from the hundred other forms of commercial relation existing between men in civil society, as to entitle the latter, in addition to receiving his legal dues from the former, to claim the right, moreover, of holding his will and conscience in pawn? To ordinary observers it looks like a mutually beneficial arrangement under which, on well-defined terms, the one lets and the other hires a certain piece of land, because each deems it his interest so to do. Whence, then, comes the notion that, besides properly cultivating the soil, and punctually paying his rent, and duly fulfilling all the other conditions of his contract, the tenant is under an obligation, whenever required so to do, to sell his soul to the devil,

I

by belying his own most solemn convictions on matters,
it may be, of vital moment to the State, in order to subserve the political interests, or, more frequently, the
mere prejudices or caprices of his landlord? And why
should such an obligation, if it exist, be assumed always
to lie on one side? I suppose that if a farmer were to
say to a landed proprietor whose land he rents, " I hire
this farm of you, I bestow upon it good husbandry, I pay
you a liberal rent for it, and I expect that at the coming
election you will vote for the man whom I shall choose
to recommend to you "—it would be regarded either as
an impertinent jest or a piece of audacious and insufferable arrogance. But why should the converse of this be
less an impertinence, or less a piece of insufferable arrogance? I am as far as possible from saying that the
only tie which should bind men to each other in society
is that of a money relation. I can perfectly well understand how a benevolent landlord, dwelling on his estates,
bestowing manifold courtesies and kindnesses on those
around him, should be so respected and beloved by his
tenants as to exercise a large and most legitimate influence over their political opinions. But the assumed
right of which I speak is a totally different thing from
this species of influence. It is claimed by men who are
neither respected nor beloved, whom their tenants know
in no other capacity than as rent-receivers and game-
preservers ; and it is exercised, not by means of superior
intelligence, kindly persuasion and weight of character,
but by means of mere brute menace, terror, and coercion.
I am afraid many of the Welsh gentry are very bigoted
believers in this sort of divine right of landlordism as
respects political matters. And this is the more unrea-
sonable on their part as they have in most other respects
left the people to shift pretty much for themselves.
Almost everything that has been done in past times for

the improvement and elevation of society in Wales has been done by the people, through their own exertions, and from their own resources, with very little help from the upper classes. I say this with no unfriendly animus to the latter; I state it as a simple historical fact, necessary to be known in order to understand their relation to the rest of the community. Some of the smaller gentry joined the early Methodists, and by their countenance and support rendered to the cause of religious revival a considerable service, which I gladly and gratefully acknowledge. Others of them have of late years taken some interest in popular education; but this has been, in many cases, so obviously subordinated to purposes of proselytism, that their very benevolence has been poisoned to the people by the infusion into it of this bitter sectarian element. With these exceptions, and looking back over the last century and a half in the history of the Principality, I am bound to say that the gentry as a class have not been the leaders of the Welsh nation in religion or morality, in education or literature, in any form of civilisation or social progress. I do not scruple to say that the heroes of Welsh civilisation must be sought, not in their ranks, but among Methodist and Dissenting ministers, giving the foremost place to that admirable body of clergymen—Daniel Rowlands, William Williams, Peter Williams, Thomas Charles, David Jones, and others, —who were driven out of [the Establishment by the excess of their zeal for the well-being of their countrymen. But the gentry as a class never understood or appreciated the full significance and value of that wonderful religious and moral revolution that was taking place around them. To this day they have not given to it more than a grudging and half-disdainful recognition, though no class, as I said in my last letter, have more profited by its social results.

I 2

And yet, while thus living apart from the real life of the nation, they have persuaded themselves somehow that in political matters they have a right to be absolute dictators, to prescribe to their countrymen what views they shall hold, what measures they shall support or reject, what candidates they shall choose to represent them in Parliament, or rather to do all this for them, and, in short, to treat them as mere serfs of the soil, who have indeed nominally the right of the suffrage, but which must never be exercised except for *their* purposes, and under their dictation.

And when this arrogant pretension is resisted they have shown a disposition—and the conflict, for reasons I have already explained, is only beginning—to employ very summary measures indeed to crush this rebellion against their will. I will take as an illustration of this the case of Merionethshire, because there the two antagonist forces of a liberal Dissenting constituency and a rampant and ruthless landlordism have been brought face to face, in a more direct manner than, perhaps, in any other part of Wales. All honour to this brave little county for the efforts it has repeatedly, though as yet unsuccessfully, made to cast off the ignoble incubus which sits astride on the heart of the Principality. It is well known that Sir Watkin Williams Wynn has large landed estates in North Wales. The residential seat of this family is in Denbighshire. For nearly two hundred years they have, almost unopposed, represented that county in Parliament. For, though the Liberals have often, and sometimes successfully, contested the second seat, conferred upon the constituency by the Reform Bill of 1832, it has always been understood, I believe, that the opposition is never against the representative of the house of Wynnstay, but against the other Tory candidate, brought forward as his associate and nominee.

Though no sort of political sympathy can exist between them and the great bulk of the inhabitants of Denbigh-shire, the prescriptive right of one of the Wynns to sit in Parliament has been hitherto tacitly admitted. But, not satisfied with this, Sir Watkin thinks himself entitled to impose his will in electoral matters upon the two neighbouring counties of Montgomery and Merioneth, whom he expects always to return some relative or creature of his. Well, at the election of 1859 the people of Merionethshire determined to make a stand against this dictatorial influence. A Liberal candidate was brought forward in the person of Mr. David Williams. The battle was fought with energy and spirit, and the Wynns triumphed. Hardly any other issue was to be expected at the first onset of the popular party, when we take into account the sort of traditional reverence long felt for the great house opposed to them, and the enormous influence of every kind, legitimate and illegitimate, which its partisans could, and very unscrupulously did, exercise. It might have been thought, however, that they would have been content with their victory. Far from it. It would appear that during the contest a few Dissenting electors—tenants of Sir Watkin and another Tory gentleman in the neighbourhood of Bala, Mr. Price, of Rhiwlas —had ventured to follow their convictions by voting for the Liberal candidate, while a considerable number more had abstained from voting, unwilling to go counter to their landlords' wishes, and unable conscientiously to support their *protégé*. So dangerous an innovation must not be tolerated for an instant. For, just think of it. Here were men—little Welsh farmers—who actually dared to believe that their souls were their own, and not the property of the landlords, and that they owed a higher allegiance to the lord of conscience than to the lord of Wynnstay. A strong blow must, therefore, be struck at once to convince them of the atrocious folly of cherishing so revolutionary and blasphemous a sentiment. What happened then? I cannot answer the question better than by giving the following extract from a letter that was published a year or two after the events described in the pages of a periodical called *The Elector*. The writer is the Rev. Michael D. Jones, one of the professors at the Independent College, Bala. He had been invited, apparently, to attend some conference on the question of the ballot, and replies thus :—

The people of Merionethshire have been brought to feel the necessity of secret voting, as the landlords, after the late election, have made those electors who refused to become their tools to smart in their material interests. The late Mr. Price, of Rhiwlas, made several tenants the object of his wrath, by turning them out of their farms. Sir Watkin in the same way, raised the rents of eleven of his tenants who had remained neutral, and ejected five that voted against the candidate he aided. Two of Mr. Price's tenants have died in consequence of this persecution, namely, Mr. Roberts, of Frongoch, the father of six children, one of which was born since his death, and his sister, who was also the head of a family. The ill-feeling that followed the election no doubt affected the health of Mr. Price, so that he also is dead. I was no elector at the time ; but I did my best to support the Liberal candidate by public speaking, canvassing, &c. My mother, aged seventy-six, was a tenant of Sir Watkin, and she lost her farm, and in January, 1861, she died. I had a chapel built upon a common, which common Sir Watkin bought of the Crown, and then sold my chapel to the highest bidder.

These facts have been frequently proclaimed in the most open manner through the Press and at public meetings, and their correctness, so far as I know, has not been questioned. There was one public meeting especially, held at Bala soon after the election, of a very significant character. It was attended and addressed by gentlemen who possess the highest reputation throughout Wales (for Bala is the seat of two of the principal Dissenting colleges), some of them men not at all addicted to political agitation, but called forth, on . that occasion, by what they no doubt felt to be the gravity of the crisis. I was greatly struck by the tone of that meeting. There was great earnestness, but no violent denunciation or abuse. On the contrary, the landlords whose conduct was called into question, especially Mr. Price, of Rhiwlas—who appears, indeed, before that access of political violence seized him, to have been a gentleman greatly honoured and esteemed by all his neighbours—were treated, not, indeed, with servility, but with singular, I might almost say, a sort of yearning tenderness. I could not help thinking while reading the report of the speeches—strange that the gentry should prefer the terrorist power they acquire by the exercise of petty despotism, which is often more a matter of pride than of any very earnest political conviction, to possessing the respect, confidence, and affection of men like these.

I have dwelt at some length on these incidents, as they may, perhaps, be regarded as typical of much that is coming. Political life, as I have said more than once, is only beginning to stir in Wales. That it will go on into fuller development I have no doubt. Whether its action shall be peaceable and prosperous will depend upon the course taken by the gentry. As I have already intimated, they may become the leaders of a loyal and enthusiastic people, if they only try to bring themselves into sympathy with their sentiments and convictions. But if they choose to adopt the high-handed policy of exacting of the people a slavish and unreasoning subjection to their will, I am convinced they are committing themselves to a conflict which is certain to be followed either by defeat or by a victory which will be to them at once ignoble and ruinous. It is vain to try to import the ideas and habits of feudalism into the light and freedom and stirring intellectual excitement of the nineteenth century. They are no longer lords over serfs of the soil, or chiefs over their clansmen, but simply men among men—men, indeed, with certain advantages of station, wealth, and superior education (presumably at least), but surrounded by an intelligent, inquiring, reading, and reasoning population. There is an old Welsh proverb, the meaning of which they ought to learn if they understood no other scrap of the language. *Trech gwlad nag arglwydd,* which may be rendered, " A country is stronger than a lord."

There are some things, no doubt, which they may do by the course I deprecate. They may render themselves odious and contemptible to a people otherwise well disposed to look upon them with a respectful and honourable regard. Some of them have already had a taste of what may come in this respect. Sir W. W. Wynn, if he is not blind to the signs of the times, must have been somewhat startled when, at the last Election, in those towns of North Wales where the appearance of a member of his family was wont to be greeted by the waving of banners and the pealing of bells and other signs of welcome and rejoicing, he found his ears saluted by a sound to which the Wynns have been little accustomed in those regions—

A universal hiss, the voice of public scorn.

Or they may drive more, as some of them have already driven many, of the best tenants on their estates— honest, conscientious, God-fearing men—to seek a refuge from oppressions and humiliations which they deemed intolerable in the United States, or Canada, or Australia, or Patagonia, and replace them by men of more supple and accommodating consciences. But they will not gain by such a substitution. They cannot expect the virtues of freemen among those who are content to be treated as slaves.

I believe I know my countrymen pretty well, and I think I could give the Welsh gentry some advice, if they could pardon the boldness of so humble an individual presuming to advise them at all, which they may with advantage lay to heart. In the first place, it would be well for them to try to acquiesce in the fact, as a *fait accompli*, that the great majority of the Welsh people are Dissenters, no longer from accident and tradition, but from deep and deliberate conviction, and to admit that it is really no business of theirs to interfere with their religious preferences. Unhappily, however, there are some of them, especially the ladies of their families— most amiable and benevolent ladies, I have no doubt, but in this matter utterly mistaking their proper *rôle*—who seem afflicted with the monomania, that it is their right and duty to choose a religion for the people, and are disposed angrily to resent the pertinacity with which they persist upon choosing one for themselves, though I have no doubt three-fourths of them are quite as competent to give an intelligent reason for the hope that is in them as those worthy lady-patronesses, who would fain have them in their leading-strings. This ceaseless meddling with the faith of the people and that of their children is doing infinite harm. It well may, and does, irritate their temper and estrange their affections ; but it does not, and will not, convert them to the Church. In the second place, it would be well for the gentry to come more directly and personally into contact with the people themselves. It is impossible to exaggerate the mischief that has been done by their being content to receive their impressions of the character, institutions, and habits of their neighbours through the medium of those who are little in sympathy with them—clergymen, lawyers, and stewards. And in passing I must say a word of this last class. It is never safe or just to direct against any body of persons a sweeping and indiscriminating censure. No doubt among stewards in Wales and elsewhere there is a great variety of character. There are some who, in fulfilling the duties of an office always, perhaps, a little delicate and invidious, do their spiriting gently, who mediate wisely and generously between their employer and his tenants, and, while protecting the interests of the former, treat the latter in a kindly and considerate spirit. But there must be others of a very different description; for there is no class upon whom the curses of the Welsh people lie so heavily—" curses not loud, but deep." In the popular satirical poetry of former days they are never mentioned but with a vehemence of denunciation which proves how intense was the indignation and abhorrence felt towards them by the popular heart. They are represented as unscrupulous, arrogant, overbearing, merciless, intercepting all rays of favour from their landlords to their tenants, and perpetrating in the name of the former, and under shelter of their authority, mean and cruel acts which—so, at least, the people fondly believed—the landlords themselves would never have countenanced had they known. How far this description may apply to any of the present race I do not presume to say ; but certainly they are not in favour, and popular instinct is rarely at fault in such matters.

But in any case I am confident it would be a great advantage if the gentry were to come into more frequent and direct communication with the people themselves. It would do them no harm to cultivate some acquaintance with current Welsh literature. There are those who have an interest in abusing their ears, who tell them that Dissenting periodicals are filled with a fierce and rabid Radicalism. It is utterly false. I have no fear as to the impression that would be produced on the mind of any candid man among them by reading these publications. They might, and no doubt would, find much with which they could not agree ; but I am greatly mistaken if they would not rise from their perusal with unfeigned respect for the intelligence, sobriety, and earnestness with which religious and political questions are discussed.

And I have a word or two to say to my countrymen— the people, and especially the Nonconformists, of Wales. If, after all, the system of terrorism and coercion is the one that shall be adopted towards them, why then they must gird their loins for the struggle. It is not possible that they should remain passive and neutral amidst the conflict of great principles, in the issue of which they and their children are so vitally interested. They may have to suffer, and if so—I say it not lightly, but very solemnly—they must be prepared to suffer. It may be as much their duty to suffer for political as it was their fathers' duty to suffer for religious freedom. And it cannot last long, nor can the result be doubtful. If they only combine in this matter as earnestly as they have done in other matters, the force opposed to them, if so we must regard it, will prove far less formidable than it seems. I say again, *Trech gwlad nag arglwydd.*

And here I must end this long series of letters. There is much more I could have said, and would like to have said ; but I have already trespassed largely on your indulgence and the patience of your readers.

It only remains for me, in conclusion, to thank you, Mr. Editor, on my own behalf and on behalf of my countrymen, for affording me this opportunity of representing them fairly to the English public. They have suffered grievous wrong in the estimation of their neighbours through ignorance and calumny. I have done my best to set them right. I love that old land that gave me birth,

> Land of brown heath and shaggy wood,
> Land of the mountain and the flood,

hallowed to me by so many tender and sacred memories, the home of my childhood's joys and the place of my fathers' sepulchres. May God bless it, and make its children virtuous, prosperous, and happy.

POSTSCRIPT IN 1883.

IT will be seen that in one of the closing paragraphs of this letter, I made an earnest appeal to my countrymen manfully to assert their political rights, even though, as was possible and probable, they might have to suffer severely for their boldness. Very nobly did they respond to that appeal in the Election of 1868. Nor did the predicted suffering fail to overtake them. Many scores of them were evicted from their farms and houses, and otherwise annoyed and tormented, for daring to vote according to their consciences. I had the satisfaction, however, of dragging their persecutors before the House of Commons and the country, and, in conjunction with others, of raising a considerable fund to relieve their sufferings. The election of 1880 completed the Liberal triumph began in 1868, and very little now remains to be done in Wales, except to maintain the position already won.

APPENDIX.

AT the Session of the Merionethshire Monthly Meeting of the Calvinistic Methodists, held at Llandderfel, Feb. 27th and 28th, the following resolution was moved by the Rev. Dr. EDWARDS, of Bala, and seconded by the Rev. E. MORGAN, of Dyffrin, and carried unanimously :—" That the Monthly Meeting here assembled desire to express their sense of the importance of the letters on the condition of Wales, which are now being published in the *Morning Star*, written by Mr. Henry Richard, and their warm thanks to him for the service thereby done to the Principality."

(Signed)   JOHN PARRY, Chairman.

AT the Quarterly Meeting of the Welsh Congregational Association of Monmouthshire, held at Berea Chapel, Blaena, on April 2, the Rev. D. Williams, the minister of the place, in the chair, the following resolution was unanimously adopted :—" That this Conference desires to place on record its most grateful thanks to Mr. Henry Richard, of London, for his able letters now in course of publication in the *Star*, on the ' Social and Political Condition of Wales,' in which, with admirable truthfulness and fidelity, he describes Welsh Evangelical Nonconformity in its origin and progress, and its relation to the moral character and religious life of the Welsh nation, thus completely disproving the ignorant and unjust charges that have repeatedly been urged against the Protestant Dissenters of the Principality. This Conference, also, deeming Mr. Richard's letters to be an invaluable means for refuting the ungenerous attacks to which the cause of Dissent in Wales is frequently subjected, begs to express its earnest hope that the excellent author will place them before the public in a separate volume."
—Signed on behalf of the Conference, by

D. WILLIAMS, Chairman.
W. P. DAVIES, Secretary.

THE GLAMORGANSHIRE EASTERN ASSOCIATION OF CONGREGATIONAL CHURCHES.—The Ministers and Delegates of the above churches having met in their Quarterly Meeting at Aberdare, on April 3rd and 4th, it was moved by the Rev. JOHN DAVIES, of Cardiff, seconded by D. E. WILLIAMS, Esq., Hirwain, and carried unanimously :—" That this meeting begs to express its high appreciation of the series of letters published in the *Star* by Mr. Henry Richard, and avails itself of the present opportunity to convey to Mr. Richard its own thanks as well as that of the entire denomination for his able exposition and advocacy of the religion and morality of the country."

AT the Quarterly Association of the Calvinistic Methodists in North Wales—representing 630 churches, 60,000 church members, and 100,000 members of Sunday-schools—held at Ruthin,

Denbighshire, April 11th, 12th, and 13th of 1866, it was unanimously resolved :—"That this Association presents its unfeigned thanks to Mr. Henry Richard for his comprehensive and excellent letters now in course of publication in the *Morning Star*, which at a timely moment give a full and accurate description of the religious and social condition of Wales, and so afford to our English neighbours the advantage of learning the truth respecting us as a nation."   (Signed)   JOHN PARRY, President.

ROGER EDWARDS, Secretary.

AT a Monthly Meeting of the Calvinistic Methodists in Cardiganshire, held at Blaenplwyf on the 4th and 5th of May, it was proposed by JOHN MATTHEWS, Esq., of Aberystwith, and seconded by the Rev. JOHN JONES, of New Quay, and carried unanimously :— "That this meeting desires to present its warmest thanks to Mr. Henry Richard for the able and excellent letters he is publishing in the *Star* on the 'Social and Political Condition of Wales,' and earnestly entreats him to publish, them in two volumes, one in English and the other in Welsh, and so secure for them a still wider and more lasting usefulness."

AT a Meeting of the Congregational Churches of Caernarvonshire, it was resolved :—" That the ministers and delegates of the Congregational Churches of the northern district of Caernarvonshire, assembled at a Quarterly Meeting held at Penter, near Bangor, on the 18th of April, having read with much interest the series of articles on 'The Social and Political Condition of Wales,' inserted in the *Morning Star*, from the able pen of their worthy countryman, Mr. Henry Richard, feel much pleasure to testify to their correctness and faithfulness, and that they bid fair to present the position of the Principality in its proper light to all English readers : and that they further beg to express thanks to the talented and indefatigable author for his noble defence of the nation's character, and to the publishers of the said journal for its circulation; with a desire to see the articles translated and published in Welsh in a collected form."

DAVID GRIFFITH, Chairman.

AT a Meeting of the Quarterly Association of the Calvinistic Methodists, held at Llandovery, Carmarthenshire, on April 25th, 1866, it was proposed and carried with great unanimity :—" That this association presents its unfeigned thanks to Mr. Henry Richard, for his able letters on the Social and Political Condition of Wales, which he has been publishing weekly in the *Morning Star*."

AT the Quarterly Meeting of the Ministers and Delegates of the Baptist Denomination in Anglesea, held at Gaerwen, on the 1st and 2nd of May, John Lewis, Esq., Vron Deg, Holyhead, in the chair, it was moved by the Rev. D. JONES, seconded by J. OWEN,

Esq., Llangoed, and unanimously passed:—"That this meeting presents its unfeigned thanks to Mr. Henry Richard for his unbiassed and excellent letters now in course of publication in the *Morning Star*, which are, to our personal knowledge of Wales, an accurate index to the present religious and social condition of the Principality. We therefore beg to express our approbation of Mr. Richard's faithful delineation and manly exposition of the religion and morality of our country."—Signed on behalf of the meeting,

JOHN LEWIS, Chairman.
JOHN PALMER, Secretary.

AT a Quarterly Meeting of the Ministers and Delegates of the Congregational Churches of Anglesey, held at Bodfford, on Monday, the 14th May, it was unanimously resolved:—"That the cordial thanks of the meeting be tendered to Mr. Henry Richard, for his very able letters in the *Morning Star* on the condition of Wales." W. JONES, Chairman.

AT the Quarterly Meeting of the Ministers and Delegates of the Independent denomination of the county of Cardigan, held at Pencae on the 22nd and 23rd ult., the Rev. Mr. Rees, Maenygroes in the chair, it was proposed by the Rev. J. M. PRYTHERCH, Llanarth, and seconded by the Rev. Mr. EVANS, Aberayron, and unanimously agreed:—"That we, the Independent ministers of this connection and others, from our knowledge of this part of the Principality, feel justified in endorsing in general the sentiments of Mr. H. Richard, of London, as stated in his letters in the *Morning Star* on the 'Social and Political Condition of Wales,' and gladly avail ourselves of this opportunity of expressing our sincere and heartfelt gratitude to the rev. gentleman for the noble manner he has espoused the cause of his countrymen in proving the utter fallacy of the calumnies which some, from whom better things could have been expected, have thought fit to libel their morals, and hope his letters will be republished in another form, both in Welsh and English, so that at last justice may be awarded to a nation which has been grossly misrepresented." T. REES, Chairman.
J. M. PRYTHERCH, Secretary.

THE South Wales Committee of the Liberation Society, having met at Crane-street Chapel, Pontypool, on Thursday, May 17th, 1866, J. Carvell Williams, Esq., London, in the chair, it was unanimously resolved:—"1. That this meeting begs to express its thorough conviction, a conviction arising from personal knowledge of the correctness of the facts and figures, stated by Mr. H. Richard in his able letters to the *Morning Star*, bearing on the morality and religion of Wales, records its high appreciation of the valuable and costly but spontaneous services which he has rendered to his much misrepresented country, and tenders him its warmest thanks ; 2. That this meeting suggests the desirableness of publishing Mr. Richard's letters in the Welsh and English languages."

THE Glamorganshire Association of Independent Churches having assembled in its annual meeting at Maesteg, May 23rd and 24th, unanimously passed the following resolution, requesting its secretary, the Rev. John Davies, of Cardiff, to forward it to Mr. Richard :—" That the warmest thanks of this Association be presented to Mr. Henry Richard for his able and exceedingly interesting letters in the *Morning Star* on the ' Social and Political Condition of Wales,' and that it deems it highly desirable to republish them in a separate form for extensive circulation through the length and breadth of the United Kingdom."

AT the Monmouthshire Welsh Baptist Association, held at Bassally, May 30th, 1866, it was unanimously resolved :—" That the warmest and most hearty thanks of this meeting be presented to the generous and patriotic Welshman, Mr. H. Richard, for the able and timely letters contributed by him to the *Morning Star* upon ' The Social and Political Condition of Wales,' in which letters the true and real condition of our country was set forth before the English public."

AT the Annual Assembly of the Congregational Churches in the counties of Denbigh and Flint, North Wales, held at Wem, June 5th and 6th, 1866, the following resolution was moved by the Rev. J. THOMAS, Liverpool, seconded by the Rev. J. THOMAS, Wem, and unanimously adopted :—" That this Conference desires to express its unfeigned gratitude to Mr. Henry Richard for the lucid, impartial, judicious, and comprehensive letters on the ' Social and Political Condition of Wales,' which appeared in the *Morning Star*, and for future reference and wider perusal urgently requests the patriotic writer to publish the same in a collected form in Welsh and English."   WILLIAM REES, Chairman.

OWEN EVANS, Wrexham, Secretary.

AT an Association of Independents held at Llanidloes, June 13th and 14th, the Rev. H. Jones in the chair, it was unanimously resolved :—" That the warmest thanks of this association be presented to Mr. H. Richard for his able letters in the *Morning Star* on the ' Social and Political Condition of Wales,' with an earnest desire that the author should republish them in a volume, to secure their permanence, and for facility of reference in time to come."

AT an Association of Baptists, held at Glynceinig, June 20th and 21st, the Rev. E. Roberts in the chair, the following resolution was passed :—" That we desire to express our gratitude to Henry Richard, Esq., for his able and timely letters in the *Morning Star* on the ' Social and Political Condition of Wales,' and our hope that he will complete his act of kindness to the Principality by collecting and publishing them in a book in a cheap form that they may have a general circulation among the people."

THE ESTABLISHED CHURCH IN WALES.*

THE Act for the Disestablishment and Disendowment of the Irish Church was one of great importance for what it did, but of still greater importance for what it implied ; for in that measure there was distinct legislative recognition of certain general principles, which are susceptible of far wider application than to the particular case they were invoked to sustain. It disposed, once for all, of the fond fantasy that the State is bound in its collective capacity to have a conscience, and in obedience to the dictates of that conscience, to impose its own creed upon the community, as the established faith of the country, to be supported by the authority, and enforced by the sanction of law. It acknowledged the principle that where an established Church never has been, or has ceased to be the Church of the nation, and fails, therefore, in its professed function as the religious instructor of the people, it has no longer any *raison d'être*, and ought to be swept away as an anomaly and incumbrance. It recognised the fact, if not for the first time, at least with more distinctness and emphasis than was ever done before, that ecclesiastical property is national property, which the nation has a perfect right through

* Reprinted from the *British Quarterly Review* for January, 1871.

K

its legitimate organ, the legislature, to apply to any purpose it may think fit, whether sacred or secular.

We need not wonder that when the Irish Establishment was abolished, men's minds should turn almost instinctively to the sister institution in Wales, as furnishing a case in many respects parallel, but in other respects still less admitting of justification. The discussion of this subject in Parliament last session, on the motion of Mr. Watkin Williams, did not take place, perhaps, under the most favourable auspices. But it was, at least, attended with this advantage, that it obliged those who oppose the Disestablishment of the Welsh Church to show their hand. As Mr. Gladstone, in addition to his many other merits as an orator, is the most accomplished debater in the House of Commons, we may safely assume that whatever could be said in defence of the Church in Wales, and in deprecation of its proposed severance from the State, was said by him with the utmost degree of plausibility and point. But certainly, on a calm review of the arguments he used on that occasion, they do not appear to be very formidable.

It may be said, indeed, that the Prime Minister made no attempt to defend the Welsh Church. He abandoned it to the strongest condemnation pronounced upon it by its adversaries, for the "gross neglect, corruption, nepotism, plunder," to use his own words, by which it has been marked; and only tried to account for these evils by laying them all to the charge of "Anglicising prelates." He admitted that, even granting what Churchmen claimed, namely, about one-fourth of the population as belonging to the Establishment—a claim, let us say, in passing, which in the face of notorious facts is wholly untenable—"the disproportion is very remarkable in the case of a Church purporting to be the Church of the nation." He admitted, moreover, as a circumstance seriously militating against the Welsh Church, that "so large a proportion of her members belong to the upper classes of the community, the classes who are most able to provide themselves with the ministrations of religion, and, therefore, in whose special and peculiar interest it is most difficult to make any effectual appeal for public resources and support." But while acknowledging all this, he resists the proposal for its disestablishment. On what grounds? First, on this ground—that there is no hostility in Wales to the Church Establishment, and that its existence does not, as in Ireland, produce alienation or bitterness of feeling between different classes of the community. But this argument, if it were well founded in fact, which, unhappily, it is as far as possible from being, does not address itself in the least to the reason or justice of the case. Even if the Welsh people were so devoid of spirit and self-respect as to feel it no grievance to have a costly Church Establishment, which exists almost exclusively for the benefit of the rich, saddled upon their necks, surely that is no proof that it is right to perpetuate the privileges of a body, whose history for generations has been marked by "gross neglect, corruption, and nepotism," and which, purporting to be the Church of a nation, does not pretend, even according to the claims of its most audacious advocates, to number among its adherents more than one-fourth of the nation. But Mr. Gladstone is wholly misinformed as to the fact. Because the Nonconformists of Wales are an eminently peaceable, loyal, and orderly people, and do not proclaim their grievances with clamour and menace, it is imagined that they do not feel the gross injustice and indignity of the position they occupy. They do feel it deeply, and they are made to feel it, by events continually occurring in their social and political life, which all spring from

K 2

this one root of bitterness. We need only refer in illustration of what we mean to the circumstances which attended and followed the last general election. Every form of unfair pressure was brought to bear upon the people to induce them to vote against their convictions, and many of those who had the courage to resist were mercilessly evicted from their holdings, or otherwise injured and persecuted. All this sprang from the existence of the Established Church, as is evidenced by the fact that in every instance—we believe without a single exception—the oppressors were Churchmen and the sufferers Nonconformists.

The other, and the only other, argument of Mr. Gladstone is this—that, except for conventional purposes, there is really no Church in Wales, that the Welsh Church is only a part of the Church of England, and cannot therefore be dealt with separately. We confess we are not very much dismayed by this difficulty ; for we can remember the time when the same reason was urged to show the impossibility of touching the Irish Church. Properly speaking, we were told, there was no Church of Ireland, but only the United Church of England and Ireland—the two Churches having, at the time of the Union, been joined together by a compact so solemn and binding that Her Majesty the Queen could not give her consent to any measure for dissolving that compact without incurring the danger of committing perjury, and bringing her crown into jeopardy. And as for providing legislation for Ireland distinct from that of England, the suggestion was scouted as an absurdity. Ireland was as much a part of the United Kingdom as Yorkshire or Lancashire, and must be governed by the same laws. The sense of justice, however, and the urgent necessities of the case, triumphed over these foregone conclusions.

There is one fact that gives a sort of sinister unity to

the religious history of Wales through all its vicissitudes. It is this : that the influence of its relations with England, whether they were hostile or friendly, whether under Saxon or Norman rule, whether in Catholic or Protestant times, has been, in this respect, uniformly disastrous. We can only glance very briefly at the proofs of this allegation. Without raising again the controversial dust which envelopes the discussion as to the time and manner of the first introduction of Christianity into this island, we may at least assume it as an admitted historical fact that early in the second century the Gospel had been planted here, and that long before the Saxon invasion there was a flourishing Christian Church in Britain. In the records of the first three or four hundred years of its existence, we find that many large collegiate establishments were formed and dedicated to religion and literature. From these institutions went forth men thoroughly instructed in the learning of their times, some of them bearing the fame of their country's piety and erudition to the uttermost parts of Europe. In the œcumenical councils summoned under Constantine the Great and his sons, in the third and fourth centuries, at Arles, at Nice, and at Sardica, to decide the great Donatist and Arian controversies that disturbed the unity of the Catholic faith, we are told that the British Churches were represented by men who bore an honourable part in the defence of sound doctrine ; for Athanasius himself testifies that bishops from Britain joined in condemnation of the heresy of Arius, and in vindication of himself. But when, in the sixth century, the Pope sent the celebrated Augustin, as a missionary, to convert the pagan Anglo-Saxon inhabitants of this island to Christianity, there came on the British Church a time of terrible persecution. Having resolutely refused to recognise the papal authority, Augustin and his

successors, in accordance with the policy of that persecuting Church which they represented, incited their
Saxon converts to make war upon the British recusants,
exasperating the national animosities, already sufficiently
bitter between the two races, by adding to it the fanatical
frenzy of religious bigotry. For many ages, therefore,
the Britons were liable to frequent incursions from their
Saxon neighbours, who, instigated by the counsels of
Rome, invaded their country, destroying their churches,
burning their monasteries, and putting to death the
pious and learned monks, who, in the seclusion of
those establishments, were pursuing the peaceable
occupations of literature and religion.* The struggle
between the ancient British Church, on the one side,
and that of Rome, backed by the Saxon sword, on
the other, continued for centuries. And when the
Saxon conquerors had in their turn to succumb to
the Norman invaders, that struggle was renewed
with greater fierceness than ever. Religion was again
unscrupulously used as an instrument of State, the
Norman princes forcing ecclesiastics of their own race
into all the higher offices of the Church in Wales, not
from any regard for the spiritual interests of the people,
but that they might aid in extinguishing the national
spirit of the Cymri, and in subjugating the country to
the Norman yoke. This policy, of course, failed, as it
richly deserved to fail. The bishops and other dignitaries
thus intruded upon the country were only safe when
surrounded by bodies of armed retainers, and whenever
the Cymric arms won a victory in the field, the interlopers had to flee to England to save themselves from
popular indignation. About the end of the twelfth
century, the Welsh princes appealed to the Pope for a
redress of these intolerable wrongs. A petition couched

* Thierry's " History of the Norman Conquest," Book I.

in eloquent language was presented to his Holiness from
Llywelyn, Prince of Gwynedd ; Gwenwynwyn and
Madoc, Princes of Powys ; Gruffydd, Maelgwn, Rhys,
and Meredith, sons of Rhys, Prince of South Wales. It
is curious, in reading this document, to observe that
some of the ecclesiastical grievances of which the British
princes complain are precisely those which the friends of
the Church in Wales are still reiterating in our own day:—

And first, the Archbishop of Canterbury, as a matter of course,
sends us English bishops, ignorant of the manners and language
of our land, who cannot preach the Word of God to the people,
nor receive their confessions but through interpreters.

And besides, these bishops that they send us from England,
as they neither love us nor our land, but rather persecute and
oppress us with an innate and deep-rooted hatred, seek not the
welfare of our souls ; their ambition is to rule over us, and not to
benefit us ; and on this account they do not but very rarely fulfil
the duties of their pastoral office among us.

And whatever they can lay their hands upon or get from us,
whether by right or wrong, they carry into England, and waste
and consume the whole of the profits obtained from us, in abbeys
and lands given them by the king of England. And like the
Parthians, who shoot backwards from afar as they retreat, so do
they from England excommunicate us as often as they are
ordered so to do. . . .

Besides these things, when the Saxons (English) rush into
Wales, the Archbishop of Canterbury puts the whole land under
an interdict, and because we and our people defend our country
against the Saxons and other enemies, he places us and our
people under judgment of excommunication, and causes those
bishops whom he sent among us to proclaim this judgment, which
they are ready to do on all occasions. The consequence is, that
every one of our people who falls on the field of blood, in defence
of the liberty of his country, dies under the curse of excommunication.

When the Reformation came, the influence of the
connection with England was, if possible, still more
disastrous on the religious interests of Wales. " The
robbery in times of peace," says Mr. Johnes, " proved
worse than the spoliation in the times of war, and the
rapacity of the Reformation was added to the rapacity
of Popery." He then describes, in language of eloquent

indignation, how the ecclesiastical endowments of the
Principality were pitilessly plundered by being bestowed
upon laymen, the descendants of the Norman invaders,
or by being alienated from the Church of Wales to endow
English bishoprics and colleges ! For the last century
and a half, again, the policy of the civil and ecclesiastical
authorities in dealing with the Welsh Church has, it
would seem, been steadily directed to the extinction of
the Welsh language and nationality by the appointment
of Englishmen to bishoprics, canonries, deaneries, and
most of the richest livings in Wales, in utter contempt
of all decency. And now when, by the legitimate operation of a State Establishment of religion, nearly the
whole nation has been alienated from the Church, so that
it has become a mere encumbrance in the land, we are
told that Wales is so inseparably united with England
that it cannot expect to be rid of the incubus until
England has made up its mind to deal with its own
Church Establishment.

But what we have to do with most especially at present is the Protestant Church Establishment in Wales,
and our indictment against it is this, that at no period of
its history has it fulfilled, in anything approaching to a
satisfactory manner, its proper function as the religious
instructor of the Welsh people. We have a chain of
testimonies in support of this allegation that are unimpeachable as to their quality, and of overwhelming force
in their concurrence and cumulation of evidence. We
are anxious to make this point clear, because the line of
defence that has been lately taken by the friends of the
Church of England in Wales is to this effect. It is true,
they say, that towards the middle of the last century the
Church had fallen into a deep sleep, and so afforded
occasion, and to some degree excuse, for the rise of
Nonconformity, which was previously almost unknown

in Wales. And then they point, in vague and sounding phrases, to a golden age that preceded that period of spiritual torpor, when the Church, alive to her high mission, ruled by native bishops, who understood the language and commanded the confidence and veneration of the country, comprehended and cared for within her ample fold the whole population of the Principality. Dissent, we are assured, is in Wales an exotic of quite modern growth, which, it is further implied, will prove to have a very ephemeral life, like Jonah's gourd, which came up in a night and perished in a night. Now all this is pure fiction. Dissent is not a thing of modern growth in Wales. It has existed more or less for more than 200 years, and whatever of vital religion has prevailed there during the whole of that period, has been owing far more to its influence than to that of the Established Church. It is not correct to say that the Church " fell asleep " in the last century, simply because it had never been awake.

And to begin with what must surely be considered as the first and most solemn duty of a Protestant Church, that of supplying the people of whom it professes to take charge with the Word of God in their own language, how does the account stand with the Welsh Established Church in this respect? Dr. Llewellyn, the learned author of the " Historical Account of the Welsh Versions of the Bible," states

That for upwards of seventy years from the settlement of the Reformation by Queen Elizabeth, for near one hundred years from Britain's separation from the Church of Rome, there were no Bibles in Wales, but only in the cathedrals or parish churches and chapels. There was no provision made for the country or the people in general ; as if they had nothing to do with the Word of God, at least no further than they might hear it in their attendance on public worship once in the week.

But how did the ecclesiastical authorities act in reference

to the translation of the Scriptures into the Welsh
language, even for use in the churches? In the year
1563, an Act of Parliament (5 Eliz. c. 28) was passed,
ordering this work to be done. In the preamble it is
recited—

> That Her Majesty's most loving and obedient subjects inhabit-
> ing within Her Majesty's dominion and country of Wales, being
> no small part of this realm, are utterly destitute of God's Holy
> Word, and *do remain in the like or rather more darkness and igno-
> rance than they were in the time of Papistry.*

It was therefore enacted that the Bible, consisting of the
New Testament and the Old, together with the Book of
Common Prayer and the Administration of the Sacraments, should be translated into the British or Welsh
tongue. The duty of seeing this done was devolved upon the
Bishops of St. Asaph, Bangor, St. David's, Llandaff, and
Hereford, and they were subjected to a penalty of £40
each if the work were not accomplished by March, 1566.
The New Testament was translated within the given
period, principally by William Salesbury, a lay gentleman, with some help from the Bishop and Precentor of
St. David's; but there was no version of the Old Testament for twenty years later, and that was done, not by
the initiative or at the instigation of the bishops, but by
the spontaneous piety and patriotism of one individual,
Dr. William Morgan, vicar of Llanshaidr-yn-Mochnant,
Denbighshire, whose name ought to be held in ever-
lasting veneration by all Welshmen. This was published in 1588. He acknowledges, indeed, that he
received some encouragement and help from the Bishops
of St. Asaph and Bangor. Ingenious apologies have
been urged for the gross neglect of the bishops in
fulfilling their commission. But Dr. Morgan, in the
Latin dedication of his Bible to Queen Elizabeth,
ascribes it to what, no doubt, was the true cause,

mere "idleness and sloth."* There was no other edition of the Welsh Bible for thirty-two years. But in the year 1620, Dr. Parry, Bishop of St. Asaph, brought out a new issue. This also seems to have been the result of individual zeal, for in his preface Dr. Parry says, that the former edition having been exhausted, and many or most of the churches being either without any or with only worn-out and imperfect copies, and nobody, so far as he could learn, even thinking of a republication, he was moved to undertake the work.† This, likewise, was exclusively for use in the churches. The first edition of the Bible for popular use was published in an octavo form in 1630, but does not seem to have originated with the Church in any way. "The honour," says Dr. Llewellyn, " of providing for the first time a supply of this kind for the inhabitants of Wales, is due to one or more citizens of London "—namely, Mr. Alderman Heylin, " sprung from Wales," and Sir Thomas Myddelton, also a native of the Principality, and an alderman of London.‡ For the next half-century there was only one edition of the Scriptures in Welsh published by Churchmen, a large folio of 1,000 copies, for the pulpits of the churches. But during the same period the persecuted Nonconformists—Walter Cradock, Vavasor Powell, Stephen Hughes, Thomas Gouge, and David Jones—published nine editions, consisting of about 30,000 copies of the whole Bible, and above 40,000 of the New Testament

* Quod idem *nostram ignaviam et segnitiem* simul prodit, quod nec tam gravi necessitate moveri ; nec tam commoda lege cogi potuerimus ; quin tam dies rex tant (qua majoris .esse momenti nihil unquam potuerit) intacta pene remanserit.

† Biblius in plurisque apud nos Ecclesiis, aut deficientibus aut tritis ; et nemine, quantum ego audire potui, de excudendis novis cogitante ; id pro irriti conatus sum in Britannica Bibliorum versione, quod fœliciter factum est in Anglicana.

‡ Nephew of Sir Hugh Myddelton, who brought the New River to London.

separately. During the subsequent half-century (from
1718 to 1769) we acknowledge with cordial gratitude
that several large editions were issued by the Society for
Promoting Christian Knowledge, [two of them at the
instigation of the Rev. Griffith Jones, and one at the
instigation of Dr. Llewellyn, a Dissenting minister. But
let it be observed that the former period, from the
accession of Queen Elizabeth to the beginning of the
eighteenth century, synchronises as nearly as possible
with the golden age which some members of the Welsh
Church fondly believe to have existed in the history
of that institution.

But let us now inquire how, in other respects, the
Established Church in Wales discharged its duties as the
teacher of the people. In the absence of the Bible, there
was, of course, all the more need for personal earnestness and activity on the part of its ministers in preaching
the word and catechising, and the regular and solemn
administration of all religious ordinances. But how was
it in this respect during the beatific period, when, as
some of the modern advocates of the Church exultingly
declare, there was " no dissent in Wales?" We will
begin our inquiries with the reign of Queen Elizabeth.
In the year 1560, Dr. Meyric, Bishop of Bangor, writes
that he had only two preachers in his diocese. Strype,
in his " Life of Archbishop Parker," describes the condition of the bishoprics of Llandaff and Bangor, one in the
South and the other in North Wales, about the year
1563, as follows. The former had been two or three
years, in effect, void, and wanted a vigilant bishop to
manage that diocese. But the great dilapidations had so
impoverished that see, that few who were honest and
able would be persuaded to meddle with it.

As for Bangor (he continues) the diocese was also much out of
order, *there being no preaching used,* and pensionary concubinacy

openly continued, which was, allowance of concubines to the clergy, by paying a pension, notwithstanding the liberty of marriage granted. . . . So that Wales being in an evil condition as to religion, the inhabitants remaining still greatly ignorant and superstitious, the Queen left it particularly to the care of the Archbishop to recommend fit persons for those two sees now to be disposed of.

In 1588, John Penry published his "Exhortation unto the People and Governors of Her Majesty's Country of Wales," every line of which was aflame with the fire of a righteous and eloquent indignation at the negligent bishops and "unpreaching ministers," to whose tender mercies his "poor country of Wales" was abandoned. We need not quote at large from the melancholy picture he gives in this and his other pamphlets of the state of the Principality in that day, as his writings have been rendered familiar to many of our readers by Dr. Waddington's "Life of Penry," and Dr. Rees's "History of Nonconformity in Wales." We will, therefore, cite only one or two pregnant sentences :—

This I dare affirm and stand to, that if a view of all the registries of Wales be taken, the name of that shire, that town, or of that parish, cannot be found, where, for the space of six years together, within these twenty-nine years, a godly and learned minister hath executed the duty of teacher, and approved his ministry in any mean sort. . . . If I utter an untruth, let me be reproved, and suffer as a slanderer ; if a truth, why should not I be allowed ?

The Rev. Henry T. Edwards, the author of a very able and vigorous pamphlet, recently published,* has permitted himself, in an evil moment, and in stress of argument and information, in defence of the Welsh Church of those days, to describe this noble-minded and devoted Christian and patriot in very opprobrious terms, as "a sour-minded Puritan, recognising no truth save in his own interpretation of the written

* The Church of the Cymry. A Letter to the Right Hon. W. E. Gladstone, M.P.

Word," &c., &c.   But Strype, at least, cannot be called
" a sour-minded Puritan."   Let us, then, revert to his
testimony in reference to precisely the same period.   In
his " Annals of the Reformation "* he makes the following statement.   We borrow Dr. Rees's summary :—

> Dr. Williams Hughes, Bishop of St. Asaph, was accused, in the
> year 1587, the year before the publication of Penry's " Exhorta-
> tion," of misgoverning his diocese and of tolerating the most dis-
> graceful abuses.   When the case was inquired into, it was found
> that the Bishop himself held sixteen rich livings *in commendam;*
> that most of the great livings were in possession of persons who
> lived out of the country; that one person who held two of the
> greatest livings in the diocese boarded in an alehouse ; and that
> only three preachers resided upon their livings, viz., Dr. David
> Powell, of Ruabon ; Dr. William Morgan, of Llanrhaidr-yn-
> Mochnant, the translator of the Bible ; and the parson of Llan-
> vechan, an aged man, about eighty years old.

We will now follow the history of the Welsh Church
into the reign of James I.   At that time there lived and
laboured in Wales a very remarkable man, the Rev.
Rees Pritchard, Vicar of Llandovery, in Carmarthenshire, the author of a work which has had a larger
circulation in the Principality than any book except the
Bible.   It is entitled " Canwyll y Cymry," or, " the
Welshman's Candle," a series of moral and religious
poems, most simple in their language, and even slovenly
in their metrical composition, but full of poetry and
feeling, and thoroughly saturated with evangelical truth.
He flourished between the years 1616 and 1644.   John
Penry, in his most vehement remonstrances, does not
employ stronger language to portray the utter ignorance,
irreligion and immorality in which the people were sunk,
than does this excellent clergyman.   But what we have
specially to do with now is the testimony he bears as to
the condition of the Church, a testimony all the more
unimpeachable as he continued through life a member

* Vol. iv., pp. 293, 294; and Appendix to vol. iv., p. 63.

and a minister of that Church.   In one of his poems,
after describing all classes as wholly given up to every
species of depravity, he adds that the clergy were asleep,
leaving the people to wallow in their sins, and to live as
they liked, unwarned and unrebuked.*   In another
poem, he puts the clergy at the head of various classes,
whom he enumerates, who were " contending with each
other, which of them should most daringly affront the
Most High."   There is evidence still more conclusive, if
possible, in the reports presented to the King by Archbishop Laud, between the years 1633 and 1638, which
are still extant among the Lambeth MSS.   This bigoted
prelate had, it seems, in those years, been specially insti-
gating the Bishops of St. David's and Llandaff to persecute without mercy those in their dioceses who were
guilty of " inconformity ; " that is, who refused to read
" The Book of Sports," and other similar obligations
which were laid on the consciences of the clergy.   After
commemorating the success with which the Bishop of
St. David's had silenced one Roberts, a lecturer, for inconformity, and reduced three or four others to submission, he adds : " He complains much, and surely with
cause enough, that there are few ministers in those poor
and remote places that are able to preach and instruct
the people." And the Bishop of St. Asaph tells Laud
that " they were not anywhere troubled with inconformity ; but that he heartily wished that they might as
well be acquitted of superstition and profaneness."
    In relation to about the same period there is still
extant an authentic and very pregnant piece of evidence,
in the form of a report by Dr. Lewis Baily, Bishop of
Bangor, as to the state of the different parishes in his

* Mae dy ffeiriaid hwyntau'n cysgu,
   Ac yn gado'r bobol bechu
   Ac i fyw y modd y mynnon
   Heb na cherydd na chynghorion.

diocese in the year 1623. There was an episcopal visitation in that year, and his description of the condition of things he found still exists in a fragmentary and mutilated form, from which extracts were published in the "Archæologia Cambrensis" (Third Series, Vol. IX., p. 283). A few extracts from this document will suffice as a sample :—

Llanfairpwllgwyngyll and Llandyssilio.—There had been only two sermons in these places for the last twelve months, which were delivered by the rector, Sir John Cadwalader.*

Penmon.—No sermon preached there five or six years last past.

Llanddona.—No service here but every other Sunday.

Llangwyllog.—No sermons at all.

Llanddeussant and Llanfairynhornwy.—The curate here is presented for not reading service in due time, for not reading of homilies, and for not registering christenings, weddings, and funerals. They had but three sermons since last Whitsuntide twelvemonth. He spent his time in taverns, was a public drunkard and brawler, quarrelling with his parishioners and others.

Llanfwrog and Llanfaethlu.—But two sermons here these twelvemonths.

And so through other counties of North Wales—Carnarvonshire, Merionethshire, Montgomeryshire. Of place after place it is reported, "There is never any preaching here," or, "There have been only two or three sermons in a twelvemonth." Of the clergyman at Aberdaron, in Carnarvonshire, it is complained that he neglected to bury a dead child, which lay in the church from Saturday to Sunday, and that when he came to the church he was drunk, and went straight from the service to the tavern.

In the year 1651, there was published a translation in the Welsh language of the once celebrated "Marrow of Modern Divinity." This translation was by the Rev. John Edwards, one of the clergy ejected by the Parliamentary Commission appointed under the Commonwealth. In the Preface, he deplores the neglect into which the Welsh language had fallen, and declares that, "among the Church clergy (y Dyscawdwyr Eglwysig), scarcely one in fifteen knew how to read and write

* In those days " Sir " seems to have been the titular distinction of a clergyman, just as " Rev. " is now.

Welsh." The reader will observe that we are following our chain of evidence link by link. In 1677, a work was published in Welsh entitled " Carwr y Cymry," that is, " The Welshman's Friend; an Exhortation to his dear countrymen for the sake of Christ and their own souls, to search the Scriptures according to Christ's command, John v. 39." This is supposed to have been written by a clergyman of the name of Oliver Thomas. The introduction is in the form of an earnest and affectionate address to " Welsh Churchmen." In this he says :—

Often does sorrow strike my heart in observing and reflecting upon the great deficiency and the utter neglect which prevail among us Welsh Churchmen, in taking pains to teach our flocks conscientiously, through our not giving ourselves with full purpose of heart to reading, to exhortation, to doctrine. We are ourselves, many of us, unskilful in the word of righteousness, and therefore incompetent to direct others. . . . Yea, my dear brethren, give me permission to say, what it pains me to be obliged to say, that in each of the Welsh bishoprics forty or sixty churches m ty be found without anyone in them on Sundays, even in the middle of summer, when the roads are driest, and the weather finest.*

We have brought our chain of testimonies down to near the end of the seventeenth century. But from that time to our own they are still more abundant.

In 1721 was published, " A View of the State of Religion in the Diocese of St. David's, about the beginning of the Eighteenth Century," by Dr. Erasmus Saunders. It contains a most deplorable picture of the condition of the Church, as regards both its material and spiritual interests. He describes some churches as totally decayed ; they

Do only serve for the solitary habitations of owls and jackdaws ; such are St. Daniel's, Castelhan, Kilvawyr, Mountain, Capel Colman, and others in Pembrokeshire ; Mount Llechryd, in Cardiganshire ; Aberllynog, in Breconshire ; Nelso, in Gower, Gla-

* " Llyfryddiaeth y Cymry," p. 211.

L

morganshire; and others in Carmarthenshire. And it is not to be doubted, but as there are districts of land, so there were originally just endowment of tithes that did belong to all those several churches; but whatever they were, they are now alienated, the churches, most of them, demolished, the use for which they were intended almost forgotten, unless it be at Llanybrec, where, I am told, the impropriator or his tenant has let that church unto the neighbouring Dissenters, who are very free to rent it for the desirable opportunity and pleasure of turning a church into a conventicle—(pp. 23, 24).

As the Christian service is thus totally disused in some places, there are other some that may be said to be but half served, there being several churches where we are but rarely, if at all, to meet with preaching, catechising, or administering of the Holy Communion. In others, the service of the prayers is but partly read, and that, perhaps, but once a month, or once in a quarter of a year. . . . The stipends are so small, that a poor curate must sometimes submit to serve three or four churches for £10 or £12 a year.

He then refers, though with great forbearance and tenderness, to the low type of character which such a state of things produced among the clergy; and then exclaims, sorrowfully, "Such is the faint shadow that remains among us of the public service of religion!"

And now (continues the author), what Christian knowledge, what sense of piety, what value for religion are we reasonably to hope for in a country thus abandoned, and either destitute of churches to go to, or of ministers to supply them, or both? Or how can it well consist with equity and conscience to complain of the ignorance and errors of an unhappy people in such circumstances? They are squeezed to the utmost to pay their tithes and what is called the Church dues (though, God knows, the Church is to expect little from it), and, at the same time, most miserably deprived of those benefits of religion which the payment of them was intended to support, and delivered up to ignorance and barbarity, which must be the certain consequence of driving away the ministers of religion, or of depressing or incapacitating them from their duty—(p. 26).

To aggravate the evils of all kinds already sufficiently rife in the Welsh Church, the English Government, about the beginning of the eighteenth century, adopted the practice, which it has continued ever since, of appointing Englishmen utterly ignorant of the

Welsh language to Welsh bishoprics.* And the bishops, following the example thus set by those acting for the head of the Church, inundated the Principality with English clergymen, their own relatives and connections, to whom all the highest dignities and the richest livings were, almost without exception, assigned. A more monstrous abuse than this it is difficult to conceive, and yet it has been persevered in for 150 years in the face of all complaint and remonstrance, and in the teeth of the express judgment of the Church itself, which declares in its 26th Article that "it is a thing plainly repugnant to the Word of God, and to the custom of the primitive Church, to have public prayer in the church, or to minister the sacraments in a tongue not understanded of the people." We need not wonder, therefore, that great prominence should be henceforth given by the friends of the Church to this, as one of the causes, if not, indeed, the sole cause, of its inefficiency and decay. How far they are justified in attaching such supreme importance to it we shall consider hereafter. But we shall for the present resume our series of testimonies to the matter of fact. Most of our readers will doubtless have heard of the Rev. Griffith Jones, of Llanddowror, the founder of the remarkable circulating schools, which, during the latter half of the eighteenth century, rendered such inestimable service to the people of the Principality. We cannot here enter upon the history of the life and labours of this admirable clergyman. If one man could have saved the Church in Wales, he would have saved it. But as Mr. Johnes has remarked with great sagacity—though he does not

* Mr. Gladstone, to his great honour, had the courage to break through this practice, by his appointment of a thorough Welshman to the diocese of St. Asaph.

appear to see the inevitable inference to be drawn from the remark—" It is a truth but too well sanctioned by experience, that a few pious ministers are the weakness, and not the strength, of an establishment, when the majority of its ministers are sunk in indifference to their sacred duties." Our object now, however, is merely to cite the Rev. Griffith Jones as a witness to the condition of the Church about the middle of the eighteenth century. In the year 1749 he published a letter in Welsh, on the " Duty of Catechising Ignorant Children and People." In that letter he observes that the

Peasantry cannot understand from sentences of deep learning in sermons the Articles of Faith without being catechised in them, which, at present, is more necessary, because there is among us such *monstrosity* (anferthwch) and such evil and barefaced craft in some places, as the frequent preaching of *English* to the *Welsh* people, not one jot more edifying or less ridiculous than the Latin service of the Papists in France. One author states that he could not help rebuking such clergymen, in spite of the spleen and wrath it was likely to bring upon him, viz., the lazy vicars and rectors, who have led a careless life from their youth, and have set their mind on keeping company, and going unsteadily from tavern to tavern, and not minding their books ; in consequence of which they are as ignorant of their mother tongue as they are of Greek and Hebrew, and therefore read the service and preach in English, without sense of shame, in the most purely Welsh assemblies throughout the country. Not much better, if any, are those who patch up a sermon of mixed language and jargon sounds, inconsonant, dark, and unintelligible, to the great scandal and disgrace of the ministry, and to the grief, damage, and weariness of the congregation.

There is one other eminent Welsh clergyman whom we must add to this cloud of witnesses before we speak of the rise of Methodism in Wales. The Rev. Evan Evans, better known, perhaps, by his Bardic name, *Ieuan Brydydd Hir*, was a man of learning and genius, a friend and correspondent of Bishop Percy and other *literati* of that age. He was especially well versed in ancient British literature, and published a Latin essay, *Dissertatio de Bardis*, containing Latin translations from the poems of Aneurin, Taliesin, and Llywarch Hen. In 1776, he published two volumes of Welsh sermons. To the first volume he prefixed a dedication to Sir W. W. Wynn in English, and an address to the reader in Welsh, in both of which he describes in bold and burning language the miserable state of the Church in Wales at that time. Here is one out of many extracts we might have given. After complaining that most of the gentry had "thrown away all regard for religion and morality," and that "the ignorance and immorality of the lower class of the people was pitiful, owing to the slothfulness and neglect of many of the clergy," he thus proceeds :

As for the clergy, such of them as still enjoy the remaining emoluments of the Church might do some good in their generation if they were so disposed. But, alas ! so little has been done by the clergy of the Established Church in this way, that there is hardly a book or a sermon left behind by any of them to testify their fidelity in their vocation, for almost a hundred years past. It is a pity they should not do something to convince the world that they are ministers of the Gospel. And it is a great pity that most of them are so *scandalously ignorant of the language* in which they are to do the duties of their function, that they can do very little to the edification of their flocks. Those who enjoy the richest benefices in the Church are most deficient in this respect, copying herein the Church of Rome very faithfully, and leaving their sheep to perish. And I am afraid that upon this and other accounts, many sincere Christians abhor the sacrifice of the Lord, who were well disposed to the Church established. And such abominations, if continued, will make it desolate !

Now, the question is what a faithful minister of the Gospel ought to do in such dangerous times. I am very sure that some conscientious ministers of the Gospel have suffered severely of late years under these lordly and tyrannic prelates. The number of such disinterested persons, it must be owned, was small, and every art and method have been used to discountenance them. If what I here aver be doubted, I appeal to the writings of the late pious and truly reverend Mr. Griffith Jones, of Llanddowror, who underwent the scurrilities of a venal priest *hired by the bishops* to *bespatter him*, though he was, by the special grace of God, without any stain or spot. By far the greater number of the clergy, like Gehazi, run after preferments, and have left the daughter of Zion to shift for herself. And his doom, in a spiritual sense, is likely to follow them and their successors.

It is well known that the man who may be called the father of Welsh Methodism was Mr. Howell Harris. He was, and continued to the day of his death, a dutiful son of the Church. He applied for ordination but was refused. He pressed his request for six years, but to no purpose. " Wherever he went," we quote again the language of a Welsh clergyman, " as a simple and unoffending preacher of the Gospel, either in the South or the North, he was denounced by the clergy from their pulpits, he was arrested by the magistrates, and persecuted by the rabble."* Now let us hear his own account of the reasons which induced him to commence and continue preaching to his countrymen. He describes his being taken before the magistrates at Monmouth, for the word of God and the testimony of Jesus Christ, and then continues—

After this, I was more satisfied than ever that my mission was from God, especially as I had so often applied for holy orders, and was rejected for no other reason than my preaching as a layman. I saw both from Scripture and the practice of the Church that the preaching of laymen was proper in times of necessity; and I thought that time of greater necessity could hardly be than the present, when the whole country lay in a lukewarm and lifeless condition. *In many churches there was no sermon for months together ; in some places nothing but a learned English discourse to an illiterate Welsh congregation;* and where an intelligible sermon was preached, it was generally so legal, and so much in the spirit of the old covenant, that should any give heed to it, they could never be led thereby to Christ, the only way to God. Seeing these things, and feeling the love of Christ in my heart, I could not refrain from going about to propagate the Gospel of my dear Redeemer.†

The second great name in connection with the rise of Methodism in Wales, was the Rev. Daniel Rowlands, of Llangeitho, a man whose powers as a preacher are described by those who knew both, to have surpassed

* "Justice to Wales: Report of the Association of Welsh Clergy in the West Riding of the County of York," p. 8.

† Morgan's " Life and Times of H. Harris," p. 41.

even those of Whitfield. The effect of his eloquence among his countrymen was extraordinary. It ran like a stream of electricity through the nation, kindling into life thousands who had been previously wrapped in spiritual torpor. Like Howell Harris, he was not merely content, but anxious, to continue his ministrations in the Church. "But he was cast out of the Church of England," says one of his biographers—the Rev. J. C. Ryle *—"for no other fault than excess of zeal." And what was the condition of the Church from which this over-zealous man was expelled by episcopal judgment ? Mr. Ryle shall answer. "This ejection took place at a time when scores of Welsh clergymen were shamefully neglecting their duties, and too often were drunkards, gamblers, and sportsmen, if not worse." †

The inference from all this has already been drawn for us by a candid Churchman. Mr. Johnes, in his "Essay on the Causes of Dissent in Wales," says that he is irresistibly led to the conclusion "that before the rise of Methodism in Wales the churches were as little attended by the great mass of people as they are now ; and that indifference to all religion prevailed as widely then as Dissent in the present day." Of the early Methodists in Wales, as, indeed, of the early Nonconformists, it may be said most truly that they did not leave the Church of their own accord. Most of them clung to it with a most touching fidelity, in spite of incessant persecution and obloquy from those within its pale, and were at last thrust out of it, for no offence but the excess of their zeal for the moral and spiritual improvement of their countrymen. It is not necessary now to put in any defence for these men ; for it has become the fashion of

* Now Bishop of Liverpool.

† "The Christian Leaders of the Last Century," by the Rev. J. C. Ryle, p. 192.

late among our Church friends in Wales, while denouncing modern Nonconformity as schismatic, turbulent, self-
seeking, and other choice epithets with which we are so
familiar in this connection, to speak with great tenderness and respect of the founders of Welsh Dissent, and
especially the early Methodists. Retaining, of course,
that *de haut en bas* air of extreme candour and con-
descension which any Churchman, however small, thinks
it right to assume when referring to any Dissenter, however illustrious for capacity and service, they do, nevertheless, admit that the men in question were admirable
men, full of genuine zeal for evangelical truth and the
salvation of souls. Nor do they scruple to deplore and
censure the perverse policy which persecuted such men
and drove them from the Church. Nay, in some cases
clergymen have even become their admiring and eulo-
gistic biographers. But this is the old thing over again.
" Ye build the tombs of the prophets and garnish the
sepulchres of the righteous, and say, If we had been in
the days of our fathers, we would not have been
partakers with them in the blood of the prophets." But
then, unhappily, by displaying the same spirit towards
the successors of these men, and branding them with
the same epithets of contumely and reproach as their
fathers applied to *their* fathers, and that for doing precisely the same work, they are witnesses unto themselves
that they are the genuine children of them which persecuted the prophets.

Having brought our review down to the great revival
of religion about the middle of the last century, let us
now inquire what the Church has done since that time
to make up for centuries of gross neglect or perfunctory
service. It might have been thought that this stirring of
spiritual life in the country, through other agencies than
its own, would have roused it, were it from no better

motive than that of jealous emulation, to make some
effort to retain or recover its influence over the population. And this, indeed, has been the case to some
extent within the last quarter of a century. But for
nearly a hundred years after the appearance of Harris
and Rowlands, during which all bodies of Dissenters
were labouring incessantly for the evangelisation of the
Principality, the Church was settled on her lees. Her
rulers not only winked at for their own profit, but
actively maintained and promoted the existence of
abuses as audacious and monstrous as ever dishonoured
a Christian Church. Her clergy, wholly abandoned to
themselves, with little or no episcopal supervision or
stimulus, were content with enjoying their temporalities
while they neglected their duties, leading lives of mere
worldly ease, and sometimes much worse lives than that.
If any reader should imagine we are indulging in exaggeration, we can refer him for exuberance of proof to
Mr. Johnes' most able and admirable work, which we
have already mentioned. It was published in 1832, and
describes the state of things then in actual existence.
The sole object of most of the alien bishops who had
been and were in occupation of the Welsh sees, seemed
to have been to provide for themselves and those of their
own households. Never was episcopal nepotism carried
to so daring an excess, with this peculiar and enormous
aggravation, that " in Wales every relation of a bishop
is in language a foreigner ; and his uncouth attempts to
officiate in his church in a tongue unintelligible to himself, can be felt by his congregation as nothing better
than a profanation of the worship of God."* As a
specimen of how the chief pastors of the Welsh Church
acted in this matter, we subjoin an extract from a speech
delivered in the House of Commons, in 1836, by Mr.

* "Johnes," p. 63.

Benjamin Hall, afterwards Lord Llanover, a gentleman whose name and memory ought to be held in grateful and honourable remembrance in the Principality, for the strenuous efforts he made in and out of Parliament to remedy many flagrant abuses in the educational and ecclesiastical institutions of the country, and to procure something like justice for Wales :—

What he complained of most was the unbounded spirit of nepotism which seemed to take possession of some of these English bishops the moment they took up this episcopal power in the Principality. He found that in the diocese of St. Asaph a relation of the late bishop held the following preferments :—He was dean and chancellor of the diocese, with the deanery house, worth about £40 a-year; parish of Heullan, £1,500; St. Asaph, £426; Llan Nevydd, £300; Llanvair, £220; Darowain, £120; Chancellorship, from fees, £400; making £3,006. Besides all this, he was lessee of Llandegle and Llanasaph, worth £600, and this all exclusive of the rectory of Cradley, in the diocese of Hereford, £1,200; vicarage of Bromyard, £500; prebend of Hereford, £50; portion of Bromyard, £50 at present, but it is expected, on the death of an old life, that this preferment will be worth £1,400. Thus he had no less than *eleven* sources of emolument, producing between six and seven thousand a-year. It appears also that his brother had about £3,000 a-year, and the total enjoyed by relations of the late bishop of the diocese alone amounts to between seven and eight thousand. But it appeared, moreover, that the amount enjoyed by the bishop, and the relations of the former bishops alone, amounts to £23,679, *and exceeds the whole amount enjoyed by all the other resident and native clergy put together!*

To what unseemly consequences the appointment of English clergymen to Welsh incumbencies must have led, our readers may conceive by imagining a number of Frenchmen installed in livings in England, and attempting to perform the service in the English language. Here are a few examples of the ludicrous scenes often witnessed in Welsh churches. They are taken from a speech delivered in 1852 by the Rev. Joseph Hughes, a very able clergyman, a native of the Principality, but residing then at Meltham :—

The mistakes (he says) that are made by Anglo-Welsh clergymen, both in the reading-desk and pulpit, are nearly as many as the words in a Welsh glossary. Some of these mistakes are of an absurd and revolting character, and subversive of that due solemnity which should be observed in the house of God. Yea, the meaning of different words and sentences of Scripture is often painfully associated in the minds of the people with those mistakes.

Before reciting these specimens, we may premise that if any of our readers should be acquainted with the Welsh language, they will immediately perceive how probable it is that the blunders described should have been committed by an Englishman trying to read Welsh, or, rather, how next to impossible it is that he should not have committed some of them.

Bishop Burgess, in pronouncing the blessing in Welsh, used to say, "The peace of God which passeth all vengeance." "Tangnefedd Duw yr hwn sydd uwchlaw pob *dial.*"

A clergyman of the name of Lewis preached at Chapel Colman, and, while speaking of man's depravity, said, "Every man is exceedingly *tall* by nature." "Y mae pob dyn yn *dal* iawn wrth natur." He meant to say blind—yn *ddall.* The little men in the congregation looked at each other with great astonishment, and seemed to question the truth of the statement. I was present at the time, and heard this as well as other mistakes.

The same clergyman, while officiating at Llandygwydd, committed the following blunder:—He made "Hail, King of the Jews," to mean "*An old cow of straw, King of Ireland.*" "Hen fuwch wellt, Brenhin yr Ywerddon."

Another, reading the words, "These things are good and profitable unto men," gave them this meaning, "These graves are good and worldly to men." "I beddau hin si da a bydol i dinion."

Another Anglo-Welsh clergyman, in his sermon quoting the words, "but the righteous into life eternal," gave them the following sense, "but to some chickens the food of the geese"—"ond i rai cywion fwyd y gwyddau."

A. B., officiating at ———, and reading the words, "let us here make three tabernacles," was understood to say, "let us here make three *pans*, one for thee, one for Moses, and one for Elias." "Gwnawn yma dair *padell.*"

A clergyman in the county of Pembroke, while reading the funeral service, made it to say, "it is sown the body of a *beast.*" "Efe a hoir yn gorph *anifail.*"

A late dean in North Wales, in repeating the following beautiful lines,

"Ymddyrcha o Dduw'r nef uwch ben,
Daear ac wybren hefyd,"

"Be thou exalted, O God of heaven, above the earth and firmament," gave them the following interpretation :—

    "*Arise, O God, above the head*
    Of two hens and the crows egg also."

    "Ymddyrcha o Dduw'r nef uwch *ban*
    Dwy iar ac *wy brân* hefyd."

Another dean, addressing his work-people at their drinkings, said, "*pori* yr ydych etto," "you are still *grazing.*" His work-people, not perceiving that the blunder was unintentional, thought their master treated them as brute beasts, and were much offended.

Another clergyman, reading that part of the "Venite," "In his hand are all the corners of the earth," said, "In his hand are all the afflictions of the earth," "*gorthrymderau'r* ddaear."

A clergyman, reading "The whole head is sick, and the whole heart faint," was understood to say, "the *back parts* are sick, and the *middle of the back faint.*" "Y *pen ol* sy glwyfus a'r *hol ganol yn lesg.*"

Another, reading "The crooked shall be made straight, and the rough places plain," "A'r gwyrgeimion a wneir yn uniawn, a'r geirwon yn ffyrdd gwastad," read it thus :—"The *crooked men* shall be made *straight,* and *the rough men* smooth ways ;" leaving the women, I suppose, still crooked and rough.

But while admitting, as who could hesitate to admit, that the practice so long followed of appointing Englishmen to all the higher ecclesiastical offices in Wales, could not fail to affect most injuriously the interests of the Welsh Church, we must utterly demur, as we have already intimated, to the exaggerated influence ascribed by the modern defenders of the Church to this circumstance, as though it were the sole cause of its inefficiency. For let us look a little more closely into the matter. The period to which the advocates of this theory are fond of reverting, as constituting the ideal era of the Established Church in Wales, when it was governed principally by native prelates is, speaking in general terms, the interval between the accession of Queen Elizabeth and the reign of William and Mary, or to take the precise dates, adopted by those among them who have most carefully investigated the subject, from the years 1558 to 1715. They specify the names of twenty-four Welshmen elevated to Welsh sees during these 157 years. But what was done by these Cymric bishops for the spiritual good of the Principality? Mr. Johnes, whose work is the great repertory of information on all matters connected with this subject, mentions three out of the whole number who seem to have distinguished themselves by some service rendered to their country. First, Bishop Morgan, who translated the Bible into the Welsh language ; but he did this *not* as bishop, but as the vicar of a small country parish in Denbighshire, and he undertook the work precisely *because* it had been neglected by the Welsh prelates to whom it had been entrusted. Second, Bishop Parry, who brought out a new edition of the Bible for use in the churches. Third, Bishop Owen, who succeeded to the diocese of St. Asaph in 1629, and of whom we are told that "he began first by his order and decrees, to establish preaching in Welsh in St. Asaph parish church, and, as it is supposed, in other parish churches in his diocese. He repaired his cathedral at his own cost, and set up a new organ in it ;" expressions which seem evidently to imply, that these very simple and obvious duties had been neglected by his predecessors, though they also were native prelates. We have, also, seen a general statement that some of the others established and endowed schools in particular localities in Wales. Of most of the rest we know nothing, but of some of them we know something. We know of Bishop Hughes, of St. Asaph, that he held sixteen rich livings *in commendam*, and left his diocese in the disgraceful condition already described in the early part of this article. We know that under Bishop Meyrick, of Bangor, there were, by his own acknowledgment, only two preachers in his diocese ; and that, according to the testimony of Strype, the grossest scandals were openly practised by the clergy. We know that the four native bishops, who by the Act of Elizabeth, of 1563, were charged with translating the Scriptures into Welsh, so neglected their duty as that even the churches were left without Welsh Bibles for twenty-five years after that date. We know that for seventy years after the settlement of the Reformation, not a single edition of the Bible in the Welsh language was issued for the use of the people. We know that from 1640 to 1690, which forms a considerable portion of the vaunted era of Welsh bishops, Churchmen published only one edition of the Scriptures—a large folio, for use in the churches—while during the same interval the Nonconformists published nine editions. We know that the contributions of the "native bishops" to the moral and religious literature of the Cymry are conspicuous by their absence. We have examined with some care Rowland's "Cambrian Bibliography" ("Llyfryddiaeth y Cymry"), containing an account of all books published in the Welsh language from 1546 to 1800, and, between the years 1558 and 1715, the era of Welsh bishops, we have failed to discover a single work written in Welsh or translated into Welsh by any one of these prelates, except "A Letter to the Welsh," by Bishop Davies, introducing Salesbury's translation of the New Testament. Nor is there any proof that they helped or promoted in any important degree the publication of religious books in the Welsh language, while the Nonconformists of that age laboured indefatigably to enlighten the people through the press. Even Vicar Pritchard's work, "The Welshman's Candle," left by him in manuscript, and which, next to the Bible, had the greatest influence on the religious character of the country, was published by the care and at the expense of Mr. Stephen Hughes, a Nonconformist minister. But above all, we know what was the state of the Church and the country during, and at the end of, the reign of this long dynasty of Welsh bishops. It is described in the language already cited of Strype, and Penry, and Pritchard, and Edwards, and Thomas, and Dr. Baily, and Erasmus Saunders, and Griffith Jones, and Howell Harris. And we beg our readers specially to observe, that all the witnesses we have summoned to depose to the character and condition of the Welsh Church during three centuries of its history, have been members of the Church itself. If there is one exception, it is that of John Penry. But he also was born in the Church, and baptized in the Church, and ordained in the Church, for we are told that he was "a famous preacher of the University;" and he had, moreover, the honour of being persecuted, imprisoned, and hung by the Church. With that one doubtful exception, all the rest lived and died within its pale. We might, of course, have added a large number of witnesses from the ranks of Nonconformity, whose testimony, we believe, would have been quite as trustworthy. But we have preferred omitting whatever might be thought open even to the suspicion of sectarian prejudice. Let us remember, that some of the " native bishops " lived several years into the beginning of the eighteenth century, and if they had exercised so blessed an influence on the Church and the country as it is now the fashion to affirm, that influence could not have suddenly vanished immediately after their death. *Nemo repente fuit turpissimus* is surely as applicable to a community as to an individual. And yet we know by the confession of all candid Churchmen, that when Griffith Jones and Howell Harris began their labours— the former in 1730, and the latter in 1735—the Welsh Church was in a most lamentable state of inefficiency and corruption.

The simple truth is, that the history of the Welsh

Church is only a crucial illustration of the invariable and inevitable evils that attend State establishments of religion. It is true that in its case these evils appear in a somewhat aggravated form, from the attempt made by the English Government to treat Wales as a conquered country, and to employ the Church as an agent in the extinction of its language and nationality. But when the life of a Christian Church is made to depend not on the faith, love, and liberality of its own members, and the presence and blessing of its Divine Master, but upon the protection and patronage of the civil government, and when, as a necessary consequence, the administration of its affairs falls into the hands of worldly politicians, who use it as an instrument of State, what can be expected but what always has ensued, that its spiritual life should wither, until those who seek real religious nourishment from its breasts are driven in sheer desperation to seek it elsewhere?

Indeed, it is curious that the friends of the Welsh Church, while enumerating the secondary causes which have led to her ruin, do not find their way, which they may do by a single step, to the right conclusion as to the primary cause from which all the others spring. Our Church, they say, has suffered grievous injustice from the alienation of her revenues, from the appointment of unqualified persons to all her highest offices, from the most flagrantly corrupt use of patronage, from the neglect of native talent, from laxity of godly discipline. But who has alienated her revenues? The State. Who has made those unfitting appointments? The State. Who has exercised patronage so corruptly? The State and its nominees, the bishops. Who has overlooked native talent? Again, the State and its nominees. Who has neglected to enforce godly discipline? Still, the State and its nominees. Yet, when it is proposed to strike away the fetters which bind them to the power that has thus maltreated and oppressed them, they hug their chains with frantic vehemence, and even use them as weapons with which to assail those who would fain assist in their liberation.

But let us now inquire into the condition of the Church in our own day. And in the phrase " our own day," we suppose we may include a period of twenty-five years. We have previously observed that, for a long time after the revival of religion which stimulated the Dissenters in Wales to such extraordinary activity in providing the means of religious instruction for the people, the Church continued sunk in utter apathy. It is impossible to find a more conclusive illustration of this than is afforded by the following statement of the comparative progress made in church and chapel accommodation during the first half of the present century. It is founded on the Census Returns of 1851, and appears in Mr. Richard's . " Letters on the Social and Political Condition of Wales," where it is cited on the authority of a very accomplished statistician, the late Mr. Plint, of Leeds. North Wales, in 1801, stood thus as to religious accommodation :—

	Sittings.	Proportion to all Sittings.
Church of England . .	99,216	. . 75·2
All others	32,664	. . 24·8
Total . . .	131,880	100·0

In the fifty years following, the population increased from 252,765 to 412,114, or 63 per cent. To have kept up the ratio of sittings to population by each of these sections of religionists, the former should have supplied 62,505 sittings, and it did supply 16,614. The latter ought to have supplied 20,576, and it did supply 217,928. The Church of England fell short of its duty 73·5 per cent., and all other denominations exceeded it 960 per

M

cent. The ratio of sittings to population, which, in 1801, was 52·1 per cent. (5·9 less than the proper standard, according to Mr. Horace Mann), was, in 1851, 88·9—that is, 30 per cent. above it.

South Wales in 1801 stood thus :—

	Sittings.	Proportion to all Sittings.
Church of England .	. 133,514	. . 61·8
All others . . .	. 82,443	. . 38·2
Total . .	. 215,957	. . 100·0

The population increased from 288,892 to 593,607, or 105·5 per cent. The quota of sittings required of the Church was 140,854 ; it did provide 15,204. The other denominations ought to have provided 86,975 ; they did provide 270,510. The Church of England fell short of its duty 89 per cent.; the other denominations exceeded it 211 per cent. The ratio of sittings to population in 1801 was 74·7 per cent., and in 1851, 84·5. Can the force of antithesis go further ?*

But we must descend a little more into detail, and furnish some practical illustrations, still taken from the testimony of Churchmen themselves, as to the condition of their Church in Wales in these modern times. In 1851, Sir Benjamin Hall made a speech in the House of Commons, in which he described the state of things at that time, especially in the diocese of St. David's. He spoke of the total neglect of archidiaconal visitations, of the small number of services performed in the diocese, and of the ruinous and deserted state of the churches. Here are a few extracts from his statements, taken, in part, from the Report of the Commissioners on Education and in part from that of a private Commissioner employed by himself to make personal investigation :—

No. 1. Kemys Hundred.—In the whole country between Fishguard on the north, and the Precelly mountain on the south, there

* This calculation does not include Monmouthshire.

is no day-school, and the state of the church exemplifies the neglect in which the population of the parishes are left. The churches of Llandeilo and Maenchlogag are in ruins. In that of Morfyl the panes of the chancel window were all out, the inside of the church wet as if just rinsed with water—indeed it had been, for the afternoon was raining.

No. 2. Hasguard.—School held in the church, where the master and four little children were ensconced in the chancel, amidst lumber, round a three-legged grate full of burning sticks, without funnel or chimney for the smoke to escape ; how they bore it I cannot tell. There had been no churchwarden in the parish for the last ten years, nor, it is believed, for a much longer period.

No. 3. Llanafan Fechan.—Mr. Rees, farmer, who lives close to the church, informed me that divine service was very seldom performed here, unless there are banns to publish, a wedding, or a funeral.

No. 4. Llandulais.—This church is a barn-like building with large holes in the roof, evincing every symptom of neglect and discomfort.

No. 5. Llanfihangel Abergwessin.—No service performed in this church five out of six Sundays for want of a congregation.

No. 6. Llanfihangel Bryn Pabuan.—Divine service not often performed here, except a wedding or funeral takes place. The vicar rides by on a Sunday afternoon, but seldom has occasion to alight and do duty, from the want of a congregation.

No. 7. Llanfair tref Helygon.—The parish church was in ruins many years ago ; the oldest inhabitant does not remember it standing.

No. 8. Llandegley.—The clergyman is forbidden to have his horses in the churchyard, but he puts in two calves. The school is held in the church, into which the belfry opens, which is open to the churchyard. Calves are still turned into the churchyard, and, I was told, still sleep in the belfry.

No. 9. Llangybi, four miles from Llanbedr College, has neither doors nor windows. The sacrament has not been administered for *ten* years. Service seldom performed at all. Cows and horses walk into the church and out at pleasure.

No. 10. Llanfihangel Ar Arth, also near Llanbedr.—Here there was once a chapel of ease ; the stones of its ruins have now disappeared, though a yew-tree marks the spot ; and the baptismal font was lately seen used as a pig-trough. Yet the Dissenters have five chapels, and congregations amounting to 1,200.

No. 11. Llandeilo Abercywyn.—The incumbent is occasionally obliged to ring the church bell himself; but sometimes the congregation amounts to two or three persons.

No. 12.—In another parish, the vicar has been in the Insolvent Court ; and was also suspended for three years for immorality, but allowed to return. He has only a congregation of about fifty, whilst the Dissenters have four chapels, with congregations of about 1,300.

No. 13. Llandeilo Fach.—No service here for about *ten* years. The roof has fallen down for several years ; but, fortunately, there is a dissenting chapel, with a congregation of about 300.

No. 15. Llanddowror.—This parish is a frightful demonstration of the destruction of the Church in Wales by the present system. About eighty years ago this parish was under the pastoral care of a native Welshman, the excellent and eminent Griffith Jones, renowned for his piety, abilities, and qualifications. This church had then 500 communicants, and people came many miles to attend the service. But this church has now no roof to its chancel, of which it has been destitute several years. The churchyard has neither wall nor fence; sheep were seen standing on the church tower some months ago. In one parish the curate has only of late been suspended, of whom the parishioners said he was " so bad the devil would soon be ashamed of him." The vicar has not preached in this parish for ten years, and lives twenty miles off. He has had the care of the parish since 1812, which is now reduced to the above deplorable state, though formerly, when in other hands, it was quoted as the model parish of Wales.

Such was the aspect of the Church in the diocese of St. David's only twenty years ago ; * and we have no doubt there were scores of other parishes in Wales in little better condition than those specified in the above extracts.

Let us now turn to look at another diocese. In the year 1850 a vigorous effort was made to promote church extension in the diocese of Llandaff. An appeal was issued in the form of a letter from the Archdeacon of Llandaff to the Bishop. The population in thirty-four districts of the diocese was 173,139. There was church-accommodation for only 17,440. Let our readers specially remark this fact. After having been in possession of the country for three hundred years, the Established Church in that part of Wales did not pretend to have made pro-vision, in the year of grace 1850, for the religious instruc-tion of more than one-tenth of the vast population com-mitted to her care. But, did the people avail themselves of her ministrations even to that extent? The answer is at hand. Among others to whom the appeal for help in building new churches, founded on the above showing, was sent, was Sir Benjamin Hall. Before responding to

* This was written in 1871.

that appeal, Sir Benjamin, who was intimately con-
versant with that part of the country, and who had his
doubts whether more church-accommodation, scanty as
it was, was really needed for the district, instructed
competent persons to count the actual numbers who
attended the churches and the dissenting chapels in
forty of the parishes of the diocese on a given Sunday.
He published the result in a pamphlet, in the form of a
letter to the Bishop, from which it appeared that, while
the sittings provided in the churches were 17,440, the
total number of actual attendants at the most numerously-attended service on Sunday, October 13th, "the
weather being particularly fine," was 7,229; while the
number which attended the 227 chapels provided by the
Nonconformists, in the same district, amounted, on the
same day, to 80,270. "From the above it appears," says
the writer of the pamphlet, "that so far from the churches
being too small to hold the remnant of Churchmen
which the zeal and activity of the Dissenters have not
wrested from us, there is, at present, room for 9,591
persons in addition to those who now attend the divine
service of the Established Church."

If we turn to one of the North Wales dioceses, that of
Bangor, it would seem that even now, notwithstanding
the energetic efforts which the present Bishop is known
to have made to infuse some life into the Church, its condition, according to the acknowledgment of its own
friends, is sufficiently discouraging. At a meeting held
in Bangor last year, the Bishop in the chair, a lay
Churchman said that Anglesey has seventy-nine parishes,
fifty-two of which have no parsonages. The seventy-
nine parishes are held by forty rectors; two of them
possess four livings each, eight of them possess three
livings each, and seventeen two each. He said that the
desirable thing for Anglesey was the residence of the

clergyman among his parishioners. He declared that
the church there was now "empty." Another of the
speakers, Lord Penrhyn, acknowledged that Dissent had
prevented Wales from becoming a heathen country. At
a clerical conference held in the same city in August,
1868, also under the presidency of the Bishop, the Rev.
P. C. Ellis, Llanfairfechan, in the course, we are told, of
"a very earnest address," made these remarks :—" He
believed if the Church of Ireland were disestablished it
would be a just judgment upon the clergy of that Church
for their shortcomings, and he was convinced that investigation would show that the clergy of the Church in this
country had fallen as far short of their duty as their
brethren in Ireland. He trembled to think what the
report of the state of the Church in Wales would dis-
close, as he believed its position was worse than that of
the Church in Ireland. If the Church in Ireland were
to go down, the Church in Wales must surely follow."

With regard to the number of persons still attached to
the Church in Wales, there is great discrepancy of opinion.
Without pronouncing dogmatically on the subject, we
propose to furnish our readers with certain data, which
may assist them in drawing their own conclusions. So
far as we know, the first, and we believe the most
careful attempt that was ever made to procure a
return of the ecclesiastical statistics of Wales, was in
1846, by Mr. Hugh Owen, Honorary Secretary of the
Cambrian Educational Society, a gentleman to whom the
Principality is indebted for many valuable services. What
provoked that inquiry was this. About that time the
National Society was making a strenuous effort to cover
Wales with day-schools, wherein, according to the
fundamental regulations of that Society, " the children
were to be instructed in the Holy Scriptures, and the
liturgy and catechism of the Church of England, such

instruction to be subject to the superintendence of the
parochial clergyman ; " " the children to be assembled for
the purpose of attending service in the parish church ; "
" the masters and mistresses to be members of the
Church of England," &c. A special appeal was issued
on behalf of Wales by Archdeacon Sinclair, with a view
" to raise a large fund " to establish schools on the above
principles. In this appeal, the suggestion " to adopt a
broad basis in which all sects could unite," was sternly
rejected. No system " from which the characteristic
doctrines of the Church of England were expunged "
could be tolerated for an instant. To show how utterly
unsuited to the country schools of this description must
prove to be, the inquiry of which we speak was
instituted. Having obtained, through means of the
relieving officers, the names and addresses of trustworthy
persons in about three-fourths of the parishes in Wales,
Mr. Owen addressed a circular to each of those persons,
requesting a return of—1. The name of every place of
worship in his district. 2. The name of the denomination to which it belonged. 3. The exact number of the
congregation at each place of worship on the first
Sunday after the receipt of the circular, in the morning,
afternoon, and evening. 4. The exact number attending
the Sunday-school at each place, morning and afternoon.* Returns were received from 392 parishes, thirty
of which were in Anglesey, fifty-nine in Carnarvonshire,

* The instructions given as to the mode of collecting the
returns are these :—" In order to fill this schedule correctly, it
will be necessary to appoint persons in whom confidence can be
placed, to count every congregation and school in the parish, and
that on the same Sunday ; not taking one place on one Sunday
and another place on another Sunday. Care should be taken not
to give account of any place in the schedule that is not within
the limits of the parish. On the other side of the schedule let all
the persons who have been engaged in counting write their
names, as an attestation of the correctness of the returns."

fifty-three in Denbighshire, seventeen in Flintshire, twenty-three in Merionethshire, twenty-eight in Mont-gomeryshire, twenty-seven in Breconshire, fifty-four in Cardiganshire, forty in Carmarthenshire, eighteen in Glamorganshire, forty-three in Pembrokeshire, and ten in Radnorshire. The population of these 392 parishes amounted to 431,000. As the total population of Wales, not including Monmouthshire, was then only 911,603, that of the returned parishes contained nearly one-half of the whole population of the country. The result is thus summarised in a pamphlet published soon after :—

From the returns it appeared that the number attending the morning services of Dissenters were 79,694, the morning service of the Church only 18,128, being more than four Dissenters to one Churchman. The afternoon services of Dissenters were attended by 63,379, those of the Church by 9,710, or about seven Dissenters to one Churchman. The evening services of the Church were attended by 5,889, and those of Dissenters by 128,216, or twenty-two Dissenters to one Churchman. The average attendance on the Sunday was—

Churchmen	· 11,242
Dissenters	. 90,415
Total average attendance .	. 101,657

Hence the average attendance of Dissenters as compared with Churchmen was as eight to one.

The actual morning attendance at dissenting Sunday-schools was 40,641, at the Church schools 3,396, or in the proportion of twelve to one. In the afternoon, the Dissenters' schools were attended by 57,243, the Church schools by 6,002, or more than nine to one, giving an average proportion of eleven to one in favour of Dissenting schools.

It may be objected that as there were probably many churches in which only one service was held, the deduc-tion, from the average of three services, may be unfair. Well, let it be noticed that the maximum number attending the churches is in the morning, when it amounts to 18,128; and that the maximum number attending the dissenting chapels is in the evening, when it amounts to 128,216; hence the ratio of the maximum attendance at dissenting chapels (evening service) to the maximum attendance at the churches (morning service) is seven to one. But leaving out of account for the moment the relative proportions of Church and Dissent, as indicated by these returns, what do they tell us of the absolute number of persons attached to the Church, as compared with the population? Instead of taking the average attendance at three services, we will, as before, take the number present at the most numerously-attended—namely, the morning service; and if we add to that number one-fourth to represent absentees, we shall have a total of 22,660 souls. This, in a population of 431,000, would amount to rather more than one in nineteen of church-goers.

But let us now turn to the official census of 1851. We have not the slightest wish to impeach the general accuracy of the facts and figures given in Mr. Horace Mann's masterly report. But the condition of Wales is very peculiar, and the general rules laid down by that eminent statistician for classifying and formulating the immense mass of figures with which he had to deal, while fair enough, no doubt, to the normal state of society in England, may not have been equally applicable to a country in so exceptional a state as Wales.

That a serious error has crept somewhere into the returns, as respects the Principality, is obvious from this one fact. The number of sittings provided by the Church of England is stated to be 301,897, and the number of the worshipping population of the same Church on the 31st of March, 1851, is stated to be 138,719. Now Mr. Mann shows that the proportion per cent. of attendants to sittings in the Established Church, throughout all England and Wales, is only thirty-three ; whereas by the above showing, the proportion of attendants to sittings in Wales alone is 40 per cent. We venture to say, that no man competently acquainted with Wales, knowing, as every such man must know, the miserably meagre attendance at hundreds of churches in that country, would for an instant believe that the churches are occupied in the proportion of 40 per cent. of attendants to sittings. Let us, however, take the figures given to us in the census. The population of Wales, including Monmouthshire, in 1851, was 1,188,914. The total number of places of worship was 4,006, which were distributed thus :—

PLACES OF WORSHIP.

Of the places of worship—
    The Established Church furnished .. . 1,180
    Nonconformists 2,826
                                    ————
            Total 4,006

SITTINGS.

Of the sittings (including estimates for defective returns)—

    Established Church furnished 301,897, or 30 per cent.
    Nonconformists . . . . . 692,239, or 70 per cent.

It appears thus, that the Church had provided sittings for only 25 per cent. of the population, while the Nonconformists had provided sittings for nearly 59 per cent.

But how about attendance? According to Table B of the Census of Religious Worship, the greatest number by very far of attendants at the services of the Established Church on the Census Sunday was in the morning. The number was 100,953. If we add one-fourth to this number for the absentees, we have 126,191, which represents 10·6 per cent., not quite one in nine of the population.

But these facts, sufficiently remarkable as they are in themselves, give really but an imperfect impression of the real magnitude of the anomaly which exists in Wales. An Established Church is presumably a *national* Church, and rests its claim to being established on the ground of its being national. Above all, it ought to be *par excellence* the poor man's Church, as some of the friends of the English Establishment are wont to allege, with what truth we pause not now to inquire, that theirs is. But in Wales the Church is not only not national, but it is anti-national; and the whole policy of its rulers for at least a hundred and fifty years has been inspired by a prejudice as stupid as it was mean, against the Welsh nationality and language. At present, of the small remnant of the population which still remains within its pale, by far the larger part are either English immigrants into Wales, or that portion of the Welsh people which have become Anglicised in their feelings and tastes; and instead of being the poor man's Church, that of Wales is emphatically and almost exclusively the rich man's Church. There are scores, we might safely say hundreds of churches, in which, if the clergyman's family and the squire's family, and their few dependents and parasites were removed, there would be absolutely no congregation at all.

Mr. Gladstone lamented, as members of the Welsh Church also sometimes profess to lament, the want of accurate and trustworthy information as to the real facts of the case as regards the several religious opinions in Wales. But whose fault is that? There would be no difficulty whatever, in a small country like Wales, in obtaining perfectly accurate information as to the number of adherents to the Church, if that body were to follow the example of the principal Nonconformist denominations in the Principality, who collect and publish periodically statistical returns of the members of their churches, and the attendants at public worship. But the clergy of the Establishment, clinging tenaciously in the face of notorious facts to the fond fancy that theirs

is the national Church, however small a fragment of the
nation really belongs to it, decline to give us the number
either of their communicants or of those who habitually
frequent their churches. We are driven therefore to
look for such incidental indications of the real state of
the case as may come within our reach. Some of these,
however, are very significant. In the National Society's
report for 1866-7 there is a return given of the number of
persons attending Church Sunday-schools in Wales. They
amounted to 49,358, or 4 per cent. of the population.
The number found in dissenting Sunday-schools, according to the printed year-books of the various denominations on the same year, was 351,128, or 29 per cent.
of the population, thus showing the Church Sunday-
scholars to be one-eighth of the entire number. These
returns are all the more valuable, because in Wales it
is not the children merely that attend the Sunday-
schools, but a very large proportion of the adult
population also.

Very striking revelations have been made, likewise, in
conection with day schools in Wales, tending to throw
much light on the actual and comparative strength of the
Church. When the Committee of Council on Education
began to make grants for the erection of schools, there
was a great rush of applicants from the friends of the
Established Church in Wales. They had many advantages in their favour for undertaking the work of establishing day-schools. They had nearly the whole land
and a great proportion of the wealth, of the country in
their possession. As they drew the means for the support of their clergy, the fabrics of the Church, and public
worship—which the Dissenters had to provide out of
their own pockets—from the national endowments, they
had all their resources at liberty to devote to the work
of education. The administrators of the national fund

were their partial friends, and dispensed it with a lavish profusion, with little or no inquiry into the fitness of those who applied, to direct and control the education of such a population as that of Wales. The National Society, as already shown, made an appeal, which was liberally responded to, for a special fund in which the co-operation of England was solicited, to promote " the education of our fellow-countrymen throughout Wales in the principles of our common Church." Our friends of the Establishment, moreover, were restrained by no scruple whatever from receiving public money to any extent for teaching their own peculiar tenets in day schools, while the Dissenters conscientiously refused the proffered grants of Government aid for religious instruction. This sudden access of educational zeal sprang avowedly in great part from proselyting motives. The late Bishop of St. David's, in one of his early charges, adverting to the peculiar condition of the Principality, confessed that the existing generation was hopelessly alienated from the Church, but that the next could and must be recovered by attending to the education of the young. The result of this effort was that State-aided Church schools sprang up in all the larger towns and villages, and in many remote hamlets, and that often in places where there were not half-a-dozen Church children.* In these schools the principles of the National Society were rigidly enforced. All the children were taught the Church Catechism, and obliged to attend church on Sundays. But State-aided schools were liable to inspection, and the inspectors had to present their reports to the Committee of Council, and these were laid before Parliament and the public. It was not possible, therefore,

* Of late years, however, the Nonconformists have taken up the question of day-school education very strenuously and successfully, so that there are at this time (1871) more than 400 British or neutral schools in Wales.

in reporting on the state of education in Wales, wholly
to conceal the fact, that an enormous majority of the
people held religious views different from those held by
the class who in many places had undertaken to direct
their education.   This has often come out in the reports
of even Church of England Inspectors.   Thus the Rev.
Longueville Jones, who was inspector of Church schools
in Wales in 1854, says:—"The number of children in
Welsh schools whose parents belong to the Church is so
very small, that it requires great experience and delicacy
of feeling to treat their young minds as they should be."[*]
As an illustration of the difficulty with which this gentleman had to contend, it is only necessary to refer to
the statistics he gives of one school under his inspection, in which out of 107 children, only five
were of parents belonging to the Church, whilst in
the following year the same school contained 144
children, of whom two only were of church-going
parents.   To come down to a later period, in the report
of the Rev. S. Pryce, Inspector of Church of England
Schools for Mid-Wales, for 1868, we find the following
admission:—"The number of children attending the
Welsh country schools I visit, is great beyond all proportion when compared with the number of persons
attending church."[†]

Among the inspectors of British Schools in Wales
was Mr. J. Bowstead.   We believe that Mr. Bowstead
was himself a Churchman.   But he was a liberal and
candid Churchman.   When, therefore, in the discharge
of his office, he began to visit the country, some
eighteen or twenty years ago, he was forcibly struck
with the singular anomaly he found to exist, of a

* Minutes of Council, 1854–5, p. 602.
† Report of the Committee of Council on Education, 1863–9,
p. 179.

large number of Church schools in some cases liberally subsidised from the public funds, and in others
supported by deductions from workmen's wages, planted
among a population of Dissenters, who felt the strongest
repugnance to much of the religious teaching forced on
their children in such schools. He had the courage in his
reports to expose this injustice, for which he became the *béte noire* of the Welsh bishops and clergy, who
often assailed him with great acrimony and conspicuous
unfairness. But, on the other hand, he had the satisfaction of knowing that he had won the enthusiastic
gratitude of a whole nation, who owe to him, in a main
degree, the exposure of a flagrant wrong from which they
had been long suffering, with little hope of deliverance.
Well, Mr. Bowstead, after extensive and careful inquiry,
in order to show the aggravated character of the anomaly
of which he complained, ventured to say that *nine-tenths
of the common people* in Wales were Nonconformists. A
writer in the *Quarterly Review* assailed him very angrily,
and accused him of " asserting without a shadow of proof
that *nine-tenths of the Welsh people* are Nonconformists." In a pamphlet issued for private circulation, Mr.
Bowstead with just severity first rebuked his assailant for perverting his words, and then showed how
little foundation there was for the charge of his having
asserted without " a shadow of proof," what alone
he did assert, that nine-tenths of the common people
of Wales, of such people as use elementary schools,
are Nonconformists. Now for the proof of this allegation. When Sir John Pakington's Committee was sitting in 1865-6, Mr. Bowstead was one of the witnesses summoned to give evidence. He had been asked
to procure the best information he could, as to the comparative numbers of children of Church people and
children of Dissenters in the schools he visited. He had

no difficulty in getting at this from the school register, because the name of the Sunday-school which each child attends is entered in a column provided for the purpose, a very satisfactory index of the denomination to which its parents belong. And what was the result? He received returns from thirty schools, " which were the only elementary schools in their respective localities." These thirty schools had an aggregate of 6,799 children under instruction, and of these 756 were returned as belonging to the Church. The children of parents attached to the Church formed, therefore, about 11 per cent. of the whole, and the children of Nonconformists constituted the remaining 89 per cent. But Mr. Bowstead supplies us with more recent evidence, which we give in his own words :—

> I have not on this occasion attempted to obtain returns from so wide an area as in 1866 ; but I have secured very complete and reliable returns, upon a considerable scale, from a locality which embraces some 20,000 inhabitants, all of whom are brought together by the industrial operations of one large company, and all of whose children, so far as they belong to the working classes, receive their education in schools promoted by that company. The locality is Dowlais, which in the matter of education is the Prussia of South Wales. It has an admirable system of schools, embracing not only unsectarian Protestant schools for the bulk of the community, but also Roman Catholic schools for the Irish. Nearly one-sixth of the whole population may be found on the registers of these schools at any moment, and I should think there is scarcely a child in the place that does not receive some amount of schooling, while those of them who stay long enough at school secure a very thorough elementary English education, together with some instruction in the French language and in drawing. I know of no place where the schools reproduce so complete a picture of the population around them, or where the free play of all the social forces presents so true a type of the characteristic features of the working men of the district.

Mr. Bowstead then subjoins a table showing the number of children belonging to each denomination, in attendance at the Dowlais schools : out of a total of 2,933, those belonging to the Established Church are

266. "The Church children, therefore, would be almost 7·7 per cent., or one-thirteenth of the whole, and the Nonconformists would claim the remaining twelve-thirteenths. This gives a larger proportion to the Nonconformists than any former return." Accompanying this return there is a letter from Mr. G. T. Clark, the Managing Trustee of the Dowlais Works, containing some remarks which are of great significance and value. In sending the tabular statement just referred to, Mr. Clark remarks:—"The proportion of the several sects may, I think, be taken as typical of the manufacturing population of South Wales and Monmouthshire." We· must quote two or three other sentences from Mr. Clark's letter :—

I see a great deal is said about the disposition of the Welsh Dissenters to allow their children to attend Church schools. We have both Church and neutral schools in this district, and I believe the Church schools of my friend and neighbour, the Rector of Gelligaer, to be as good as any semi-rural schools in Wales, and they are largely attended by the children of Dissenters. But this is not from love of the Church, but because they desire education, and the district has no other schools. The Welsh in this respect, like the Scotch, have a craving to get on, and they will make a sacrifice to educate their children ; and if the only accessible school be a Church school, to it they will apply. They trust, and safely trust, to the domestic example, and to the Sunday teaching in the chapel and chapel school, to keep the children in the special faith of their parents. . . . Those who say that the South Wales manufacturing population have a regard for the Church of England speak in utter ignorance of the matter. Their dislike to the Church, as an Establishment, is very strong, and is yearly becoming stronger.

It would be difficult to find a more competent and trustworthy witness. Mr. Clark is himself an attached member of the Church of England. He is a gentleman of rare intelligence, who has for many years been at the head of one of the largest and best conducted of the great iron works of South Wales. His knowledge of the population of the whole district is extensive and accurate.

N

His testimony, therefore, as to the comparative number of Churchmen and Dissenters, and the feelings of the Nonconformists towards the Establishment, must be held to be unimpeachable.

But what is the comparative progress in accommodation for worship made by the Church and the Nonconformists since the Census of 1851? We have the materials for an approximate estimate. The Bishop of Llandaff, in his charge, delivered in August, 1869, states that, since 1849, the number of new churches erected in his diocese is thirty-nine, not quite two churches in the year; and the number of churches rebuilt on the same site, but whether enlarged is not stated, is thirty-six, making a total of seventy-five. Against this we have to place the following return, furnished to us in detail, but of which we can here give only a summary, of what has been done in the same diocese by three Nonconformist bodies since 1850 :—

Number of new chapels built by the Independents . . 68
Number of ditto rebuilt and enlarged 46
                                                — 114
Number of new chapels built by the Baptists. . . 66
Number of ditto rebuilt and enlarged 39
                                                — 105
Number of new chapels built by Calvinistic Methodists . 52
Number of ditto rebuilt and enlarged 42
                                                — 94

Total 313

Let it be observed that this showing includes only the three principal Nonconformist denominations, as we have failed to procure returns of the different bodies of Wesleyan Methodists and other minor sects, which would make undoubtedly a considerable addition to the total increase of dissenting accommodation. And yet how does the comparison stand even with such incomplete elements as we possess? We find that the Noncon-

formists have built 186 new places of worship against
thirty-nine built by the Church, and have rebuilt and
enlarged 127 more against thirty-six rebuilt by the
Church.

With regard to the whole of Wales, our information as
respects what the Church has done during the last
twenty years, is not so perfect as we could wish. The
number of new churches built in the four dioceses
appears, as nearly as we can calculate from the data
within our reach, to be about 110. But there is more
difficulty in getting at those rebuilt and enlarged, as in
one of the returns (that of St. Asaph) we find churches
" restored " and " improved "—words implying merely
repairs of existing fabrics without any additional accommodation—mixed up with those which have been " rebuilt and enlarged." We have the precise number
rebuilt, and we are willing to presume somewhat enlarged, in Llandaff, which is thirty-six, and in Bangor,
which is thirty-one. We think it would be a liberal
allowance from the statistical report before us to assign
thirty-five " enlarged " churches to St. Asaph, and,
judging by the number of new churches built in ·St.
David's, we presume that thirty " enlarged " churches
would cover all that has been done in that diocese,
making a total rebuilt and enlarged of 132. Let us now
turn to the Nonconformists. The following are facts on
the substantial accuracy of which our readers may rely.
Since 1850, the Calvinistic Methodists have built 321
new chapels, and have rebuilt and enlarged 435 more,
providing additional accommodation in all for 123,881
worshippers, at a cost of £366,000. The Independents,
during the same period, have built 118 new chapels, and
have rebuilt and enlarged 200 more, furnishing additional
accommodation for 130,000 at a cost of £294,000. The
Baptists have built 142 new chapels, and rebuilt and

enlarged ninety-nine more, furnishing additional accommodation for 81,800, at a cost of £163,000. Thus, these
three denominations alone have in twenty years built
581 new chapels, and rebuilt and enlarged 734 more,
providing accommodation for 308,681 persons, at a cost
of £823,000.

But it must be further observed, that it is not merely
in the matter of religious instruction that the Nonconformists have become almost exclusively the leaders of
the Welsh people. As respects literature and science,
and all important social and political movements, it is
the same. The literature of Wales, and not its religious
literature merely, is almost wholly Nonconformist.
There are about thirty periodicals, quarterly, monthly,
and weekly, at present published in the Welsh language.
Of these all but three are owned and edited by Dissenters. There are nine commentaries on the whole
Bible, and nine besides on the New Testament alone,
some original and some translated from English, and
only two of these were done by Churchmen, and even
they were Dissenters when they began their work.
There are eight Biblical and Theological Dictionaries,
and as many bodies of divinity or systems of theology,
and no Churchman, we believe, has had a hand in the
production of any one of them. There is a History of
the World, a History of Great Britain, a History of
Christianity, a History of the Church, a History of the
Welsh Nation, a History of Religion in Wales, all by
Dissenters, besides elaborate denominational Histories of
the Calvinistic Methodists, the Independents, the Baptists, &c. Indeed, all the ecclesiastical histories in the
language are Nonconformist, and all the general histories
except the History of Wales, by the Rev. Thomas Price,
and a small work called the " Mirror of the Principal
Ages." There is a valuable work, illustrated by many

excellent maps and diagrams, entitled " The History of
Heaven and Earth," treating of geography and astro-
nomy, by the Rev. J. T. Jones, of Aberdare, formerly a
Nonconformist minister. There is another large geographical dictionary in course of publication by a Dissenting minister. There are two copious Biographical
Dictionaries edited and principally written by Dissenters.
There is now, and has been for several years, in course of
publication an Encyclopædia in the Welsh language
(Encyclopædia Cambrensis), dealing, as such works do,
with the entire circle of human knowledge. It was
described by the late Archdeacon Williams, who had
seen the earlier volumes, as " a work of great promise,
as sound in doctrine as it is unsectarian in principle."
It is studiously free from denominational taint, and was
intended to be a great national undertaking, the contributors being indiscriminately selected from the ablest
writers of all denominations, the combined learning and
talent of Wales being thus engaged in its preparation.
The enterprising publisher at the outset addressed a
letter to all those among his countrymen, of whatever
Church or creed, who had distinguished themselves in
any way by their literary acquirements and productions,
inviting their co-operation. We have now before us a
list of the contributors, amounting to ninety names, and
out of these ninety, there are certainly not more than
nine Churchmen.

The English public has of late years become partially
acquainted with a remarkable institution existing in
Wales, which has come down from very ancient times,
called Yr Eisteddfod, or the Session, meaning in its
primitive signification the Session of the Bards. Its
object is to encourage the cultivation of literature,
poetry, and music. Prizes ranging from £1 to £100 are
offered for the best compositions in poetry, prose, and

music. The highest honour bestowed by the Eisteddfod is the Bardic chair, and the productions entitling the successful candidates to this distinction are supposed to possess rare merit. There are now living nine chaired bards, of whom one is a clergyman, seven are Nonconformist ministers, and one a Nonconformist layman. In musical compositions the proportion would be about the same. And certainly the Welsh clergy of the present day have not, any more than their predecessors, distinguished themselves as authors. A catalogue of Welsh books published within the last twenty years would show a very " beggarly account " standing to the credit of the official instructors of the Welsh people.

Such are the past history and the present condition of the Established Church in Wales. Surely no legislature with any sense of justice can long refuse to deal with so anomalous an institution as that we have described. A Church which has wholly failed, and is still failing, to accomplish the only object for which it pretends to exist, from which—and that entirely owing to its own criminal neglect—the great body of the people are hopelessly alienated, and which has no vital relation with the religious, political, social, or literary life of the nation, is not merely a theoretical anomaly. It is an intolerable practical grievance, and is becoming more and more so every day. For its friends, numbering as they do nearly all the landowners and wealthy classes, galvanised, of late years, into a sort of spasmodic zeal, which is far more political than religious, are making frantic efforts to regain for their Church the ascendancy it has so righteously lost, by a very unscrupulous use of their wealth, their social position, and their control over the land. The advocates of the Church, especially in the English Press, are trying to wreak their vengeance on a nation of Dissenters, by traducing the character of the people and ridiculing their language, their literature, and their religious institutions; and this they are not deterred from doing by their utter ignorance of all three. Some of the Welsh clergy, also, exasperated by seeing their pretensions contemned and their ministrations forsaken, are propagating the most monstrous calumnies against their successful rivals, the dissenting ministers. One Conservative journal in London has especially distinguished itself by throwing its columns open to these anonymous slanderers. Here are some of the flowers of speech that have been plentifully scattered in its pages on the Welsh Nonconformists. "The Welsh language is made the instrument of evil by preachers and other supporters of anarchy and plunder." "The people are actively taught to commit arson and murder; they are regularly drilled into Fenianism." "Dissenting ministers are the curse of Wales; there is scarcely a sermon or lecture they deliver that is not full of sedition."

And yet the country whose population is thus systematically trained to sedition and murder is more free from serious crime than any part of the United Kingdom; so free, indeed, that in many of the counties the annual visit of Her Majesty's judges is almost a work of supererogation. Take as an example the county of Cardigan, which was the scene of the most extensive and cruel political persecutions after the last Election, where many tenants were evicted from their holdings, or otherwise injured, some of them under circumstances of a singularly exasperating character. And yet at the Assizes, that were held immediately after, there was not a single prisoner to be tried. Mr. Justice Hannen, n charging the grand jury, said "that a perfectly clear calendar was a circumstance he had never before met with since he had been on the bench, and he understood from his brother judges that only in the Principality of Wales was such a thing known, and that there it was frequent. Whether it was attributable to race or to the influence of religious teaching, he could not say, but he felt deeply interested in the matter, and whatever might be the cause, there was the indisputable fact, one of which the county of Cardigan might well be proud."

These insane efforts to drive or to drag the people back into the Church by coercion and calumny produce, of course, precisely the opposite effect. Indeed, the Conservatives, in their treatment of Wales, are triumphantly vindicating their right to the title bestowed upon them by Mr. Stuart Mill, as "the stupid party." Unhappily, however, they do succeed in embittering the heart of the people, and in introducing alienation and anger into their relations with the classes who are thus tempted to tamper with their religious and political rights. And all this is owing to the existence of an Established Church.

WELSH EDUCATION

AND THE

ESTABLISHED CHURCH IN WALES.*

SOME time ago a gentleman, connected with a college in
Wales, wrote to a Welsh Member of Parliament to ask if
it were not possible to obtain a set of all Parliamentary
Papers relating to Wales for the library of the institution
in which he was interested. The answer, after due
inquiry, was that there *were* no Parliamentary Papers.
relating to Wales. There would be no difficulty, it was
said, in furnishing a vast and voluminous collection of
Blue Books about Ireland, or Afghanistan, or Turkey, or
South Africa, or Egypt, or Syria, or wherever tumult.
and disorder prevailed. But Wales was conspicuous by
its absence from the roll of these ponderous documents.
Some one has said, " Happy is the nation that has no
history." But that saying proceeds on the old assumption that history consists, to use the words of Carlyle,.
" of a series of intrigues and butcheries and battles ; "
and these are the things that for the most part find their
way to diplomatic and Parliamentary records. But in
all healthy communities there are developments of
national life continually going on, of a far more important
and lasting character than any inscribed on the pages of
" drum and trumpet history." So has it been with the
Principality of Wales. Though, happily, for several

* From *The British Quarterly Review* for April, 1883.

centuries it has had little of blood and glory to chronicle
in its annals, it has not been without a modest history of
its own, though not of a nature to find its way into Blue
Books, or to figure much in Parliamentary debates. For
a century and a half it has been quietly working out its
own destinies, material and moral, in the seclusion of its
picturesque valleys, and under the shadow of its everlast-
ing hills, diligently cultivating its soil, rearing its thousands of cattle and horses, and its myriads of sheep to
help in feeding and clothing its more luxurious neighbours; extracting from its exhaustless mineral treasures
the coal and iron and lead and silver with which it has
so largely enriched the nation; excavating whole mountains into slate and stone quarries, whose produce has
gone forth into all the markets of the world; and con-
structing docks, harbours, railways, tramroads, and
canals to convey these resources of its soil and fruits of
its industry into almost all quarters of the globe. During
the same period it has not neglected its inner and higher
life, but has built thousands of houses dedicated to the
service of God, within whose walls a larger proportion of
its people are habitually gathered for purposes of religious
instruction and worship than perhaps can be found in
any part of the kingdom.

It has done much, also, for the education of its people;
first by a system of Sunday-schools, the most perfect
that ever existed in any country, and then by such rapid
multiplication of the means of elementary education as
to have provided, according to the last report of the
Committee of Council, no fewer than 1,705 schools and
departments of schools, besides colleges of various kinds,
on which, within thirty years, at least £150,000 have
been expended. Nor has it been wanting in intellectual
activity, for it has created a large living literature, comprising works of sterling value in history, biography,

poetry, music, science, natural history, natural and moral philosophy, besides calling into existence and into extensive circulation a copious assortment of periodicals in the form of reviews, magazines, and newspapers in both languages.* To which must be added that it has in a humble way cared not a little for the æsthetic culture of its people ; for by its Esteddfodau and Cymmrodorion societies, it has diffused through the whole country a passionate love of poetry and music, and has brought, and is bringing, to light the treasures of bardic and legendary lore which had been stored up in its ancient language and literature.

At last, however, Wales has an entire Blue Book of more than a thousand pages all to itself, to the no little gratification of its simple-minded people, who have been inclined to bewail, and almost to resent, the previous absence of themselves and their country from these pretentious official records.

O fortunatos nimium sua si bona norint!

---

* In a very able and exhaustive paper on " The Literature of Wales," read at the Church Congress in Swansea, in 1879, by the Rev. David Williams, the following statement was made : " Wales has 62 newspapers and 22 periodicals in the proportions of 32 Welsh to 52 English. Deducting the metropolis with its 4,000,000 inhabitants, and 505 newspapers and 619 periodicals, England, with a population fourteen times as large as Wales, had only thirteen times as many newspapers, viz., 1,162, and hardly seven times as many periodicals. Ireland, with four times the population, has only a little more than twice the number of newspapers, viz., 148 to our 62; while the 174 of Scotland make the two countries proportionately equal. In periodicals Wales stands at the top of the ladder ; Scotland has 41; Ireland, 29 ; England, 148 ; Wales, 22. Thus in proportion to population Wales has twice as many as England, one and a-half as many as Scotland, and four times as many as Ireland." Mr. Williams adds, with honourable candour, " The native press is almost entirely in the hands of the Dissenters. The adherents of the Church of England in Wales stand in the same proportion to the population as her publications do to those of Nonconformity. Out of 32 Welsh periodicals the Church claims the significant number of four." (" Report of Church Congress," pp. 557, 558.)

In August, 1880, the Government appointed a Commission, or Departmental Committee, as it was called, "to inquire into the present condition of Intermediate and Higher Education in Wales, and to recommend the measures which they may think advisable for improving and supplementing the provision that is now, or might be made, available for such education in the Principality." This committee consisted of Lord Aberdare, as chairman, Viscount Emlyn, M.P., the Rev. Prebendary Robinson, H. Richard, Esq., M.P., Professor Rhys, and Lewis Morris, Esq. It is important to note the constitution of this body. Five of its members were Churchmen, of whom one was a dignitary of the Established Church and a high official in the Charity Commission, and another was a Conservative member of Parliament and heir to a peerage. There was only one Nonconformist. When we consider that this was a body appointed to inquire into the educational condition and requirements of a community the overwhelming majority of whom are Nonconformists, it must be admitted that it was not unduly in favour of the latter. It is understood that while the project was yet in a state of incubation, and the list of names was privately circulated about, a respectful representation was made to the Government on this point, with a view to a more equitable distribution of parts. But little heed is ever paid to the wishes and remonstrances of Nonconformists, whatever party is in power.

The inquiry appears to have been elaborate and exhaustive, the Committee sitting to receive evidence in many of the principal towns of Wales and Monmouthshire, beginning with Holyhead and ending with Newport. No one can charge, or has charged them, so far as we know, with showing any partiality to Nonconformists in the selection of witnesses. So far otherwise, that the

number of Churchmen called was far in excess of the
proportion which the adherents of the Church bears to the
population of the country. If, therefore, there was any
primâ facie ground for jealousy, it would surely lie with
the majority, who might have thought themselves insuf-
ficiently represented on the Committee and in the witness-
box. Happily, however, the gentlemen to whom the work
was entrusted were men of an eminently honourable
temper, who kept their minds open to evidence and to
the conviction which evidence produces, and who prosecuted their work with a candour and a conscientiousness
which merit grateful acknowledgment.   And none
deserve this tribute of admiration and gratitude more
than the Rev. Prebendary Robinson, whose death,
hastened, we fear, by the laborious part he took in this
inquiry, is a serious and almost irreparable loss to the
party of liberal thought and generous sympathies in the
Church of England.

The Report of the Committee has been favourably
appreciated by the Government, which has already acted
upon several of its recommendations, and intends, it is
understood, to propose other measures very much in
accordance with its remaining suggestions.   It has also
been received with general satisfaction and approval
throughout the Principality.   The only exception has
been a certain class of the clergy, who seem to have been
sorely troubled by the presence of the one Nonconformist
on the Committee, and the part he took in the inquiry.
In the last number of *The Church Quarterly Review*
vent is given to the feelings of that class in a singular,
and certainly not a very saintly, fashion.   We must
explain to our readers the grounds of the grievance
which these poor, persecuted people urge against the
delinquent Commissioner.   Mr. Richard appears to have
entered upon his duty by assuming, what at first sight

does not look a very irrational principle, namely, that in
providing a scheme of education for Wales or any other
country, it is important that it not only should be sufficient in quantity and efficient in quality, but that it
should be of such a character as to command the confidence of the great body of the people for whom it is
intended. Now, in Wales, as in England, the great
bulk of the educational endowments, especially of
grammar-schools, whatever may have been the conditions of the original trust, have fallen into the hands of
the Church of England ; for, according to the interpretation of the Court of Chancery, it was made a presumption of law that when no explicit direction was
given in reference to religious matters in the will of the
testator, the religious instruction was to be according to
the principles of the Church of England. So Nonconformists were almost cut off from all share in this great
inheritance of the past. The Endowed Schools Act of
1869 was partly intended as a remedy for this wrong.
By the 17th section of that Act it was provided that, in
future schemes for endowed schools (excepting those
where by the express terms of the foundation directions
for instruction of a denominational character are imposed), religious opinions and attendance or non-attend-
ance at any form of religious worship shall not in any
way affect the qualification of any person to be a member of the governing body. But Nonconformists have
found nearly everywhere that this provision, with an
appearance of great liberality, is, in its practical working,
almost wholly illusory. For the schemes are so mani-
pulated, that what with feoffees and nominated and co-
optative Governors and other contrivances, the enormous
preponderance is always secured to Churchmen on the
governing bodies, and they, of course, elect the masters
and decide the character of the schools. That was

found to be the case in Wales. With two, or possibly three exceptions, they all come ostensibly under the operation of the 17th section of the Endowed Schools Act already referred to. To quote the words of the Committee in their Report :—

It may, therefore, be fairly assumed that the Welsh grammar schools are generally, so far as regards their legal status, undenominational. But while legally and nominally undenominational, they are, with few exceptions, practically in the hands of one religious body, which constitutes what is comparatively a small minority of the population. We found during the time of our inquiry that in several instances the whole of the governing body were members of the Church of England. That was the case at Ruthin, Cowbridge, Monmouth, and the two endowed schools for girls at Llandaff and Denbigh ; and even in those cases where Nonconformists are represented on the governing body, the overwhelming majority generally belonged to the Established Church. Thus at Bangor, out of twenty governors, only four are Nonconformists ; to which must be added that the headmaster and most of the other masters are almost always members of the Church of England.

A very flagrant instance was given in the evidence of Mr. Richard Davies, the Member for Anglesea. In Beaumaris there is a grammar-school with a large endowment, one of the richest foundations in Wales. Mr. Davies had taken pains to ascertain the religious profession of the population of Anglesea, when he found that there were 35,000 adherents of the Nonconformist Bodies out of a total population of 49,000. How many of the remaining 14,000 belong to the Church of England there are, so far as we know, no data to determine. In any case the disparity of numbers was sufficiently striking. But in such a population as the above there was not a single Nonconformist on the governing body of the endowed school.

Now, is it natural, is it credible, that the Nonconformists of Wales should be satisfied with such a condition of things, satisfied, that is to say, that, in order to secure for their children any share of the benefits

accruing from the educational endowments of their
country, they must send them to schools governed by
Churchmen, taught by clergymen, and surrounded by an
ecclesiastical atmosphere calculated to alienate them
from the faith of their fathers? They were *not* satisfied
with such a condition of things. The evidence on this
point was absolute and overwhelming. The words of the
Commissioners are :—

> It was the unanimous contention of Nonconformist witnesses
> that the fact of the governing body and the teaching body
> belonging to one religious denomination gives a denominational
> character to the school. . . . It appears to us that this con-
> tention has some foundation in fact, and that a preponderance of
> Churchmen, for instance, on the governing body of any school
> might, for anything by way of safeguard to be found in the
> scheme, lead to the conversion of the school into what would
> practically be a Church institution.

There were some of the older witnesses who explained
and justified this " watchful jealousy " on the part of the
Nonconformists, by referring to the deliberate and determined attempt made some thirty or forty years ago in
Wales to seduce the children of Dissenters into the
Church, by imposing on the country the National school
system of elementary education in its most drastic form
of ecclesiastical bigotry, including compulsory learning
of the catechism and compulsory attendance at Church
services and Sunday schools. And they further em-
phasised their objection by alluding to the " divers and
strange doctrines," especially those tending to under-
mine Protestant principles, now current in the Church,
with which they did not want their children's minds to
be contaminated.

Now, the indictment against the Nonconformist member
of the Committee is, that he asked questions calculated
to bring out these facts and opinions, instead of allowing
them to remain in the shade, and that so he disturbed
the comfortable *status quo.* But was it open to Mr.

Richard to take any other course without betraying his trust? He was bound by a twofold obligation—one to his Nonconformist countrymen to see that their views and wishes were fairly represented to the Committee, and another to the Government, to take care, so far as he could, that they should not be left under misapprehension on a matter of such vital importance to the efficiency of any scheme they might hereafter propose for advancing intermediate education in Wales.

It is important in this connection to specify some of the facts which were brought to light in course of the inquiry. According to a very moderate estimate, there are 15,700 boys in Wales and Monmouthshire requiring an education higher than elementary. It was found that to meet this want there are twenty-seven endowed grammar-schools, with aggregate endowments of £12,788. It was found that the whole number of boys attending these schools was only 1,540. It was found that the accommodation was largely in excess of the number in attendance. It was found, to quote the words of the report, " that whereas three-fourths of the population, according to some estimates, and a larger proportion according to others, are Nonconformists, the returns showed that two-thirds of the scholars attending the grammar-schools were members of the Church of England." It was found that the explanation offered by some witnesses to account for this—namely, that among the upper classes in Wales Churchmen largely predominate—does not meet the case, seeing, as the report again says, " that the upper classes in Wales do not, as a rule, send their sons to the provincial grammar-schools, and that the majority of the scholars were the children of smaller professional men, farmers, and tradesmen, classes that are understood to be largely Nonconformist." It was found further that Nonconformist

O

parents often send their children to schools at a distance, and at a probably greater expense, rather than send them to the endowed grammar-schools in their own immediate neighbourhood.

Now here is a series of rather curious facts that surely require some elucidation. And if Mr. Richard asked questions which served to throw light upon them, was he not rendering a real service to the object for which the inquiry was instituted? One of the points expressly indicated in the letter of instructions constituting the committee, which was addressed by the Noble President of the Council to Lord Aberdare, as requiring special attention, was this, that "it had been represented to Her Majesty's Government that, at the very best, the exist- ing educational institutions [in Wales] of a class above elementary schools, are not only insufficient in number, but so inconveniently situated, and in some cases so *fettered by denominational restrictions* as to be at once in- adequate to meet the wants of the Principality, *and unsuitable to the character of the population."* But if it is meant to insinuate that the feeling of the Nonconformists in this matter was elicited only by " leading questions " from Mr. Richard nothing can be further from the truth. As soon as the appointment of the Com- mittee became known, conferences and meetings were held in various parts of Wales, and resolutions were passed and ordered to be laid before the Committee, in which the question of the unsectarian character of the education required for the country was put in the forefront as of the most cardinal importance. Thus a deputation appeared at Aberystwith, to present a series of resolutions adopted at a Nonconformist confer- ence held in that town which, they stated, was " largely attended by people from all parts of Wales," where " all the Nonconformist denominations were represented, and might be taken as fairly representing the Nonconformist opinion throughout the Principality." The first of those resolutions was this : "That all existing endowed grammar schools in Wales and Monmouthshire should be made perfectly free from all religious restrictions in their governments, appointments, scholarships, and ex-hibitions." Resolutions from other representative meet-ings were also presented to the same effect. And cer-tainly the only Nonconformist member of the Com-mittee would have been guilty of a gross dereliction of duty if he had failed to bring into prominence a point of such vital moment as this.

But some of the clergy are hardy enough to contend, against the emphatic testimony of the Nonconformist witnesses and the unanimous opinion of the Commis-sioners, that it is no grievance that Dissenters should have to send their children to what are practically Church schools ; that they do not feel it to be a grievance, or, if they do, it is because they are ignorant or bigoted or priest-ridden. There is something sufficiently ridiculous in finding a class who are officially and socially separated from the great body of the people, thus pronouncing *ex cathedrâ* against the explicit declarations of the people themselves, speaking through their most intelligent and trusted representatives. We have heard a story of a gentleman going into a shoemaker's shop to buy a pair of boots, and having, after infinite straining and pulling, got his feet into one pair where they were held as in a vice, inflicting upon him the acutest agony, he begged the shoe-maker to pull them off at once. But the conceited votary of St. Crispin, instead of doing that, assured him with a smiling face that it was a beautiful fit, that it was a great mistake to imagine that they hurt him, or, if they did, he was only to wait a little while and it would be all right. The unfortunate victim, limping and grimacing about

the shop, and appealing in vain for relief, was so exasperated with the man's pertinacity and grinning
self-conceit, that in the extremity of pain and passion he
knocked his tormentor down. We do not advise our
Welsh Nonconformist friends to do that. But we do say
that they have a right to know and to declare for themselves where the shoe pinches. " *We* have not heard
these complaints," exclaim these clerical oracles. But
does it never occur to them to reflect that the Nonconformists are not likely to make *them* their confidants in a
matter of this sort, that the Welsh farmer or tradesman
or dissenting minister would hardly choose to whisper
his grievances into the ears of the Bishop of Llandaff or
the Dean of Bangor, still less into those of the clerical
masters at the head of the endowed grammar-schools.
And is it not curious that religious teachers, who ought
to understand and even to encourage a certain scrupulous
sensitiveness of conscience on matters of religion, should
expect from others concessions on questions of conscience,
which it is very certain they would indignantly repel if
exacted of themselves? We observe that the audacious
Dissenting Commissioner ventured occasionally to put to
some of the clerical witnesses a question on this point, in
the form of an *argumentum ad hominem.* Thus, referring
to the scruples of Dissenters as to sending their children
to Church schools, he asks one dignitary of the Church:—

You do not consider that that feeling is altogether an unreason-
able one ; or, to put it in this way :—If we could suppose the conditions entirely reversed, and if in all the grammar schools of
Wales the head master was almost always a Dissenting minister,
and always a Dissenter, and all the other masters were Dissenters, and the majority of the boys were on a Sunday marched
to a Dissenting chapel, and the head master conducted family
worship as a Dissenter, you, as an earnest clergyman of the
Church of England, would not strongly recommend Churchmen
to send their children to such a school, would you?

Of course, when the question was put in that form the

worthy clerics were a good deal embarrassed. The simple truth is that our Church friends have been so long accustomed to ecclesiastical and social ascendency that they seem stricken with an absolute incapacity to con-· ceive why Nonconformists should feel just as Churchmen would feel under similar circumstances. That *they* would deem it a great oppression to conscience, if they were obliged to have their children educated by dissenting ministers and under dissenting influence, is most certain. But, then, it is a mere piece of impertinence for Noncon- formists to indulge themselves in the luxury of keeping a conscience, as respects the education of *their* children.

But besides asking inconvenient questions, there are two other things by which Mr. Richard has given deadly affront to the *Church Quarterly* Reviewer. One of them is this. His colleagues had recommended that in the reorganisation of old, or in the establishment of new intermediate schools, "any provision made for religious instruction shall be confined to the reading and explanation of Holy Scripture, and shall not include instruction in the formularies of any Church, sect, or denomination." Differing from them on this point, and on this point only, Mr. Richard proposed as a sub- stitute for the paragraph just cited, these words—

In view of the objection of principle felt by many to the appli- cation of public money to the support of religious teaching of any kind, and the extreme difficulty of finding any form of Scriptural teaching which would have much religious value, out of which everything must be excluded that would offend, not only members of the Church of England and the various bodies of Nonconfor- mists, but Roman Catholics, Jews, &c., we are inclined to recom- mend that in schools receiving grants from public sources the instruction should be confined to secular elements, the duty and responsibility for the religious training of the children being left to the parents and to the ministers of the different denominations to which the parents belong, care being taken that in school arrangements sufficient opportunities and facilities should be afforded for that purpose. In a country where the doctrines and observances of religion are held in such high and universal estimation as they are in Wales, there would be no danger that the religious instruction of children would be neglected if it were left to the care of the parents and pastors. This plan would also be attended with the advantage that the Conscience Clause, with all the humiliations and heart-burnings to which it gives rise, would be altogether dispensed with.

In a Memorandum attached to the Report, Mr. Richard develops his views more fully by pointing out how "the religious difficulty," which has been found perplexing enough in connection with elementary education where all public aid is restricted to day shcools, would be very seriously aggravated if similar aid were given to boarding schools. He therefore suggests that intermediate schools that are to receive grants from public funds should be day schools, as is universally the case in the United States. Or, if boarding schools are to be subsidised, it should be either, as is done in Ireland, by a system of prizes, exhibitions, and certificates to students, on examinations out of which all religious subjects are excluded, or, as previously indicated, by confining the instruction to be given to secular elements.

I hope it is not necessary for me to say (adds Mr. Richard) that I make this suggestion not because I am hostile or indifferent to religious instruction as a part of education. No one can have a deeper sense than I have of its paramount importance. But I have a sincere conviction that the plan I recommend will best subserve the interests not only of religious equality but of religious education. I have very little faith in the efficacy of a religious teaching out of which everything definite and positive has been eliminated, in deference to conscientious denominational susceptibilities. If the proposed " explanation of Holy Scripture " be of such a nature as not to offend the conscience of any body of religionists, it will be so minimised and attenuated, so deprived of all significance and vitality, that it can be of no great value to impress the intellect, the affections, or the conscience of a child. And thus parents may be deluded into the belief that the children are being religiously educated, when, in fact, they are only fed on the husks of vague and jejune generalities little adapted to exercise a deep and lasting influence on life and character.

It is curious enough that at a diocesan meeting of Churchmen held in the chapter-room of Bangor Cathedral, with the bishop in the chair, a resolution was passed formally approving and endorsing "the judgment of the senior member for Merthyr Tydvil," as to the expediency of making, as regards all new colleges, first grade and second grade schools, the "common ground of the college and school purely secular." And in a public meeting held in the same city, the venerable bishop of the diocese, quoting the latter words of Mr. Richard, adds, "I perfectly agree with Mr. Richard in what he has thus laid down."

But what exasperates the writer in the *Church Quarterly* is Mr. Richard's allegation, that the doctrines and observances of religion are held in high and general estimation in Wales, and that therefore the people are not likely to neglect the religious instruction of their children, if that were not given in day schools. When you find a poor and scattered people like the Welsh, providing out of their poverty the means of religious instruction and worship for themselves as they have done; when you find that within a hundred years they have built at least 3,500 places of worship,* the support of which, and of those who minister in them, is supplied by their willing contributions; when you find them raising annually for these and similar purposes some £400,000, surely that may be taken as a tolerably fair presumption that they *are* a people who hold the doctrines and

* My honoured friend, Rev. Dr. Rees, of Swansea, who is more thoroughly acquainted with Nonconformist matters in Wales than any man living, writing to me in regard to this statement, says :—" Your statement that the people of Wales have built within a hundred years 3,500 places of worship is greatly below the mark. There are now no less than 4,233 Dissenting places of worship in Wales. About 400 of these may be only schoolrooms, where, however, regular services are held ; but 90 per cent. of the existing chapels have been entirely rebuilt within the last fifty years, and several of them built for the third time. You would not have exaggerated if you had stated that 6,000 chapels had been built in the last hundred years."

observances of religion in high and general estimation.
And has it never occurred to this writer to inquire or to
reflect what would have been the present condition of the
Principality, grossly neglected as it has been for several
centuries by Church and State, if there had *not* existed
among the people a general regard for the doctrines and
observances of religion? But the writer before us will
admit no such inferences to be drawn. On the contrary,
Mr. Richard has again outraged his delicate sensibilities
in this very matter.

In a lecture on "Nonconformity in Wales," which he
delivered at the Memorial Hall, he referred, as one would
think it was not very unnatural he should on such an
occasion, to the number of chapels that had been built by
the voluntary liberality of the people, as some evidence
of their religious earnestness and zeal. The Commissioners also in their Report refer to this in terms of
kindly recognition.

It is indisputable (they say) that Nonconformity in Wales is
the outward expression of deep-seated religious convictions
among the people. The Welsh, turning aside from the ecclesiastical system recognised by the State, have created their own
and maintain it at a large annual cost voluntarily incurred. They
have reared their chapels everywhere, on the lonely hill-side no
less than in the populous town, and by this means and through
their Sunday-schools, which seem to keep a life-long hold over a
large part of the population, an almost universal interest in
religious questions is maintained.

But this is intolerable to the Reviewer. Of course he
cannot dispute the fact as to the multiplication of chapels.
He cannot annihilate the hard material fabrics which
stand up sturdily before his eyes in solid bricks and
mortar, or more frequently in granite or limestone, and
obstinately refuse to disappear. But what the Reviewer
will do, or try to do, is this. He will show, as he says,
from the testimony of Nonconformists themselves, first,
that the chapels are frequently built from unworthy

motives, and are sometimes left heavily burdened with
debt; and, secondly, that the influence of the chapels
and Sunday-schools, so far from having produced the
salutary moral and religious effects ascribed to it by Mr.
Richard and the Commissioners, has on the contrary
generated spiritual torpor, religious dissipation, and
general immorality !

How does he make this good on the testimony of Nonconformists themselves ? We will explain to our readers
how. He has ransacked, or got some one to ransack for
him, the pages of dissenting religious periodicals for the
last thirty or forty years for the materials out of which
to construct this indictment of self-condemnation. And
what is the character of the materials thus discovered ?
Well, thirty years ago—for nearly all the quotations are
of that date—there were some good men " jealous with
a godly jealousy " for the spiritual interests of the
churches, and writing with the *perfervidum ingenium* of
their race, who directed attention, in perhaps not very
measured language, to certain dangers which they apprehended were appearing among them. Chapels were
sometimes unduly multiplied under the influence of
sectarian zeal or personal ambition, without due regard
to the heavy debts left upon them. There might be too
great a fondness for the mere hearing of sermons, lectures,
and speeches, the excitement attending which might be
mistaken for genuine religious emotion. Early and
constant familiarity with the words and doctrines of
Scripture might lead men to lose a due sense of their
Divine authority. It was complained that at the period
referred to, that is, thirty years ago, there was much
spiritual torpor, out of which it behoved the churches to
rouse themselves in order to contend against the encroach-
ments of Popery and Mormonism, in regard to which
there was a temporary panic in Wales, arising as respects

the former from what was thought the alarming spread
of Popish doctrine in the Church of England. Sincere
and salutary warnings like these, such as may be found
in the religious literature of any Church at any time in
the history of Christianity, from apostolic days down-
wards, are heaped together as proofs of the deplorable
condition of Welsh Nonconformity, and capped with the
triumphant exclamation from the writer, "Such is the
testimony of Dissent itself." The wonder is that the
treasure-trove which rewarded his charitable quest
amounts to so little.

But that is not all. From the same, and from some
other sources, there is a second series of extracts referring
to certain evils, which, in spite of the exertions of all
religious bodies, still existed in the country to an extent
that deeply grieved all true Christians and patriots. At
the time in question, that is, about thirty years ago, the
Temperance reformation was being prosecuted in Wales
with great force and fervour. As was very natural, the
promoters of that movement dwelt, with no doubt somewhat exaggerated emphasis, upon the magnitude and
extent of the evil against which they were contending.
As the agitation was taken up almost exclusively by the
dissenting bodies, the periodicals of the Nonconformists
denounced the sin of drunkenness, and bewailed its prevalence in the country in language of great vigour and
vehemence, and with an unguarded latitude of expression
which was then the besetting sin of our worthy teetotal
friends. About that particular period also great prominence had been given to another form of evil, which,
owing to certain reprehensible traditional customs existing in the country, was supposed to be specially prevalent in Wales—that arising out of the relation of the
two sexes. The Report of the Commissioners on Education, published in 1847-48, which, instead of a faithful

picture, was a hideous caricature of the state of the country, had dwelt upon this with most unfair exaggeration in order to make good their favourite allegation, that unchastity was " the peculiar vice of the Principality." There are facts enough to prove that it was not, and is not so. But the accusation had the effect of arousing all the religious bodies to additional intensity in denouncing the evil, which they did with an earnestness amounting almost to agony. " Let ministers of the Word," so runs one of the quotations, " deacons of churches, the whole body of religious members of every denomination, teachers of Sunday schools and children, heads of families, one and all, awake, and then this plague will be driven away from the country." Well, the Reviewer has diligently picked out all the tit-bits he could find bearing on these matters from Nonconformist publications of thirty years ago.

But what will our readers say to this, that the writer in the *Church Quarterly* actually ascribes the evils, so solemnly bewailed, and so vehemently denounced in the dissenting periodicals, *to the influence and operations of Nonconformity ?* We are willing to hope that it was done inadvertently, without his being fully aware of the significance of his own language. But that such is the only construction that his language bears is undeniable. In introducing his quotations, he uses these words—

We will proceed to cite from the " Drysorfa," the " Dywy-giwr," and the " Seren Gomer," which are respectively connected with the Calvinistic Methodists, the Congregationalists, and Baptists—the three leading denominations in Wales—a few of many of their own statements. . . . in order that *our readers may be enabled to judge for themselves what was the real influence of Welsh Dissent* a few years ago, and unless the contrary can be proved, may be presumed to be its condition at present also. We would not say its *results*, probable or necessary, for that is beyond the scope of our inquiry.

And at the end of his quotations, the latter part of which

relates exclusively to ·the drunkenness and incontinence which the writer insinuates—though, we believe, most untruly—to exist in an aggravated form in Wales, and referring to the statement made by Mr. Richard, in his lecture at the Memorial Hall, as to the remark- able multiplication of chapels in Wales from 993 in 1816 to 2,826 in 1851, the Reviewer writes, putting his words for greater emphasis in italics, " yes, there were 2,826 chapels *at the very time when these revela- tions of the inner workings of Dissent were made by dis- senting writers."*

The most necessary and ·most painful part of our task, therefore, remains; that is, to vindicate the character of Welsh Nonconformists, and of the Welsh people generally, from the cruel imputations and in- sinuations of their assailant. It is unfortunate for the members of the Church of England in Wales that they seem to think it necessary for their case to blacken the reputation of their countrymen—to extenuate their virtues and to exaggerate their vices as much as pos- sible. The reason of this is not far to seek. For a long time they attempted to deny, or conceal the fact, that the great bulk of the Welsh people had forsaken their Church and become Nonconformists. But, unable to resist the cumulative evidence as to the fact, they think the next best thing is to assure their English friends that Nonconformity, so far from having been a blessing, has been a bane to the country, since those who live under its influence are an ignorant, depraved, and degraded community. There is something cowardly as well as cruel in the means taken to effect their pur- pose. It is not done in Wales and through the medium of the Welsh language, for the facts are there too well known, so that the calumny would soon be smothered by an overwhelming refutation ; but it is proclaimed in the pages of English newspapers and periodicals, and thus the poison percolates into channels where it is scarcely possible that the antidote can reach. The mode of attack adopted by these accusers of the brethren is also singularly disingenuous. They fasten upon some general statement, as to the marvellous progress that has been made in the Principality in intelligence, religion, and morality within the last hundred years, progress which it would be gross ingratitude to God and man not thankfully to recognise, and they affect to believe that this is intended to claim absolute immaculacy or perfection for its social condition. They know well enough that no such claim is made. But it is convenient to assume it, and then they set themselves to rummage among all the garbage of crime and vice which exist in every country, and, dragging these to the surface, they exclaim triumphantly, or at least suggest such an exclamation, to their many English readers, " Such are your intelligent, religious, and virtuous people of Wales ! "

And, first, let us say a word as to the question of chapels and their debts, which seem to be severely exercising our worthy friends of the Establishment in these days. The line taken by the members of the Church of England in Wales on this subject is very peculiar. They acknowledge that they have failed absolutely to provide in any adequate degree the means of spiritual instruction for the people of the Principality ; that if every seat in every church were occupied, there would still be tens, if not hundreds, of thousands without any accommodation for public worship; that but for the exertions of Nonconformists large tracts of the country would be in a state of heathenism. And this is the case, let it be observed, after they have done their utmost. For some thirty years ago the members of the Church in Wales did

put forth considerable efforts to make up for ages of past
neglect. These efforts have been gladly and gratefully
recognised by the Dissenters. To quote words used by
Mr. Richard himself, in a speech he delivered at
Wrexham, in April last, reviewing the past fifty years
in the religious history of the Principality, and referring
to the great improvement in the Church of England,
during that time :—

> We have seen dilapidated churches repaired or rebuilt, and a
> considerable number of new ones erected ;. we have seen services
> more frequent, and conducted with far more spirit and devotion ;
> we have seen among the clergy able and earnest men, devoted to
> the duties of their office, abounding in activity and labour, ready
> to go forth into the streets and alleys to compel the careless to
> come in, and not unwilling, if they meet any stray lambs
> wandering out of or near the fold of Dissent, to take them up and
> carry them in their bosom.

In the diocese of Llandaff especially, where indeed the
need was most urgent on account of the rapid and
sudden growth of the population, there was, on the
accession of the late bishop, a praiseworthy effort made
to supply the grievous deficiency in the services of the
Church of England. A Diocesan Church Extension
Society was formed, and with liberal help from the
Ecclesiastical Commissioners and other extraneous
resources, considerable results were obtained. The
cathedral, which " for 127 years had been a roofless
ruin," was restored ; new churches and new parsonages
were built, and old ones repaired ; curates were multiplied, and services were reformed and made more regular.
Yet how fitful, feeble, and inadequate were all the exertions made, is shown by the report of the Society's
operations, presented at its annual meeting in 1879, and
which is thus summarised in the *Church Times* :—

> It was established in 1851, for the purpose of enabling the
> Church in the diocese to increase its accommodation, and to
> multiply its clergy in proportion to the enormous growth of the

population in the great mining districts of the diocese. The society was vigorous in its birth. In its first year it had an income of £5,112. But of this sum nearly £4,000 was given in the form of donations. However, in 1852, it had an income of £1,598. From that year down to the present—if we except the years 1863 and 1868, in which spasmodic efforts were made to rescue the society from ruin by the galvanism of such a demonstration as that which we are now noticing—the income has steadily decreased until the total receipts for the year had fallen from £5,112 in 1851 to £942 in 1878.

During this period the population of the diocese has been increasing at the rate of 8,000 a year, and has more than doubled itself during the life of the society. Thus, while the resources of the society have been steadily decreasing, the fields in which it ought to operate have been continually growing. A more melancholy state of things it is difficult to imagine.

The writer in the *Church Times* then calls attention to a memorial that had recently been presented to the bishop by some of the Welsh clergy, in which

They point out that two of the seven sects in Glamorganshire alone have 118,000 adherents, and that of these no less than 110,000 worship in the Welsh language, and contribute more than £40,000 per annum to religious purposes. . . . The sum of £942 contributed for church extension by all the Churchmen of an enormously wealthy diocese contrasted with more than £40,000 per annum given by the Welsh Dissenters in one county of the diocese, is painfully significant.

There are other remarks by the Church journalist still more pungent which we withhold, though we might be justified in producing them, by the example set by the Reviewer in his quotations to the disadvantage of Dissent, from Nonconformist publications.

Such being the acknowledged inefficiency of the Church to provide for the spiritual wants of the people, and such being the exertions and sacrifices of the Nonconformists to supply its lack of service, our Church friends nevertheless are never weary of carping and cavilling at the latter, and trying to depreciate in every possible way the work they are doing.

Misrepresentations of the grossest nature are continually made as to the circumstances under which chapels are built in Wales. Mr. Gathorne Hardy, now Lord Cranbrook, once stated in the House of Commons that they were built, not from voluntary contributions for Church purposes, but merely as matters of profitable investments, yielding often as much as 7 per cent. When this was contradicted by the member for Merthyr, Mr. Hardy, like a true Christian gentleman, publicly withdrew his statement, and expressed his regret that he had been misled into making it.   Shortly after, the *Press* newspaper, which was then the recognised organ of the Conservatives, declared that chapels in Wales were built by employers of labour, and held in mortgage by them for sums advanced for their construction, and that pains and penalties were inflicted oh those of the people who refused to frequent or encourage these chapels.   This preposterous statement, which awoke peals of laughter in Wales, had nevertheless to be refuted in England. Quite recently there appeared in the *Guardian* a speech which had been made at a Diocesan Conference, by the good Archbishop who has just passed away from us, to this effect, that the sale of advowsons in the Church of England differed nothing in principle from the system which prevailed in Wales, where men bought shares in chapels in order to place in them as ministers persons in whom they were interested.   When this was denied on the best authority, the charge was varied by an anonymous writer into this form : the case of a Nonconformist gentleman, or body of gentlemen, buying or building a chapel, and solely by virtue of their money-power exercising the patronage by placing in such a chapel a minister whose ministry they had reason to believe would not be a moral and spiritual, but a commercial success. When this grossly offensive allegation was again contradicted in the most positive and peremptory manner, and the evidence in support of it demanded, the libeller again shifted his ground into the safe general assertion that some of the chapels in Wales were heavily laden with debt.

But the favourite allegation is that chapels are built from "unworthy motives." No one will deny that chapel-building, like everything else human, is sometimes promoted under the influence of very *mixed* motives, where an alloy of the gross earthly elements comes in to adulterate what ought, no doubt, to be altogether heavenly. It may be frankly admitted, and indeed is constantly admitted and bewailed by Nonconformists themselves, that places of worship are unduly multiplied under the promptings of sectarian jealousy or emulation. But it is most edifying to remark the cool assumption of our worthy Church friends, that it is only Nonconformists who are afflicted with these infirmities of the flesh. Yes, *they* indeed, if they are Christians at all— which in the exercise of a large and liberal charity they may be admitted to be—are Christians of a very defective and immature character. But pass over to the other side, where Churchmen are drawn up in array, and you are at once among the spirits of just men made perfect The one class may be seen fluttering with soiled and heavy wing among the beggarly elements of this world, the others have soared into the pure empyrean—

> Where bright aerial spirits live insphered
> In regions mild of calm and serene air,
> Above the smoke and din of this dim spot
> Which men call earth.

We are asked to believe—or, at least, so much is implied—that *they*, when they build or enlarge churches, are actuated by simple disinterested regard for the good of man and the glory of God. Why, nothing is more perfectly notorious, that scarcely a church has been built in Wales for the last forty years that has not been built really, and often openly and avowedly, in rivalry to Dissent. Indeed, in many parts of that country there is nothing else for the clergy to do but to convert or pervert the people from Nonconformity to the Church. The members of the Church of England do not attempt to disguise, and we honour them for their frankness, that their object is "to regain to the Church the Welsh people,"* and so they do not scruple to become, in a spiritual sense, "robbers of churches," provided they are only Nonconformist churches. "Let them babble and bleat," said the Bishop of Winchester at Swansea, "if they will only feed in our pastures and come home to our sheep-folds." We do not blame them very severely for this. But let us have equal measure. If the aggrandisement of one's own Church be "an unworthy motive" for building places of worship when it is done by Dissenters, how does it cease to be so when done by Churchmen?

And now as to the moral condition of the country. The whole tendency of this article is to blacken its character in order to discredit Dissent. But how does the matter stand? Look first at the criminal statistics of Wales. A few months ago Mr. Justice Williams stated that he had just been on the South Wales circuit; that he had been to Cardiganshire, Carmarthenshire, Pembrokeshire, Breconshire, and Radnorshire, and that in all those five counties there were only two prisoners to try, one of whom was acquitted, and the case of the other was disposed of in half an hour. Mr. Justice Lindley went to North Wales. In Merionethshire there was not a prisoner to try, nor one civil case. In Anglesea not a prisoner to try, nor one civil case. In Denbighshire there was one prisoner, who was acquitted, and one civil case, which was settled without a trial. In Flintshire there were seven cases to try, but of these,

* Canon Lewis at the Swansea Church Congress.

judging by their names, three were Irish. Of the seven,
three were found guilty, and of the three who were convicted two were sentenced to two months' and one to
three months' imprisonment. In Carnarvonshire there
were five prisoners. Two or three years ago Mr. Justice
Lush, addressing the grand jury at Swansea, said it was
highly creditable to South Wales that there were only
seven prisoners for trial, notwithstanding that the
calendar now represented the whole of the business of the
South Wales counties. Would it not be natural to suppose that all Welshmen, at least, would be proud of such
a record as this, and regard it as honourable to the
character of their countrymen? But there is hardly
any passion so mean and malignant as ecclesiastical
jealousy. And so we find Welsh Churchmen doing their
utmost to pooh-pooh this evidence of the social virtues
of the population, trying in every way to reduce its
significance. The paucity of crime, we are told, is
owing to the fact that the population of Wales is almost
exclusively a rural population. In the first place, this
is not true as a matter of fact; and in the second
place, if it were true, have we not ample and appalling
evidence thrust upon us daily that the most deadly
crime may abound in purely agricultural districts? But
why should this be? While English judges are year
after year expressing their delight and astonishment at
maiden assizes or the lightness of the calendar, and
paying the highest tribute to the " purity of conduct,
the good morals, and the honesty of purpose which dis-
tinguish the Principality "—to use the language of the
late Lord Chief Justice Cockburn—why should the
dignitaries and clergymen of the Church of England be
anxiously endeavouring to deprive their countrymen of
any special credit in the matter? The reason evidently
is this. The great bulk of the people are Noncon-

formists, and may not their remarkable freedom from
crime be ascribed to the influence of Nonconformist
chapels and Sunday-schools? But that must not be
allowed. Rather than that, better blow upon this
social peculiarity as meaning nothing in reality that is
deserving of admiration or respect.

We come next to the question of temperance. Very
obviously the effect, if not the intention, of the
article in the *Church Quarterly* is to convey to English
readers the impression that the Welsh are an exceptionally drunken people. The Reviewer quotes, *more
suo*, a few passionate sentences which appeared thirty
years ago in two Nonconformist periodicals bewailing
the prevalence of intemperance. He then takes a more
recent extract from an English paper published at
Cardiff, containing one of those fanciful statistical
calculations which, as has often been said, may be made
to prove anything. Seven licensed houses were selected
in Swansea and Merthyr Tydvil, and the number of
persons who entered them during one hour on one
Sunday evening was counted. To these were added the
numbers *assumed* to enter at other hours. Then the
number of all the licensed houses in Glamorganshire was
taken, and multiplied by the number which were assumed
on the above very slender basis to frequent the seven,
and the grand total was announced as a proof of the
addiction of the Welsh people to Sunday drinking. This
grand total amounts to 100,000! That is to say, that
one-fifth of the whole population of Glamorganshire—
men, women, and children—are made to spend their
Sunday evenings in public houses! We do not scruple
to say that it is a preposterous calculation, wanting in
nearly all the elements required for a sober and trustworthy conclusion. The Reviewer then refers to the
Sunday Closing Act for Wales, passed in 1881, but

which has only just come into operation, and adds the following offensive insinuation— "Whether the voluntary movement which led to this result originated *in a consciousness that such a measure was specially needed for Wales*, or from a sympathy with the efforts that were made elsewhere, we do not venture to decide." We have no idea what is meant by "the efforts made elsewhere;" but we happen to have an official document which will throw considerable light on the suggestive doubt of the writer. It is a Parliamentary return, showing the number of convictions from September, 1879, to September, 1881, of all persons arrested for drunkenness on Sunday in England and Wales. And the result is this, that the convictions in England were *ten* per 10,000 of the population; the convictions in Wales were *four* per 10,000. This is for all Wales; but if we omit Glamorganshire, which the writer before us does when it suits his purpose, where, as Sir Thomas Phillips said more than thirty years ago, what is still truer now, " there are found large numbers of Englishmen and Irishmen, many of them driven thither by crime and want, and characterised by much that is lawless and unrestrained," the proportion of convictions in Wales is only 2¹/₇ per 10,000 against the ten per 10,000 in England.

The answer to the innuendo grounded on the demand for the Sunday Closing Bill was given by anticipation in the debate on that measure in the House of Commons, and by no less a person than Mr. Gladstone, whose generous sympathy for Wales is requited by the deepest gratitude and veneration :—

The Welsh (he said), as far as I have ever had the means of judging, are upon the whole, and especially as you come among the poor Welsh, a very sober people. You may say that if they

P 2

are a very sober people they are less in need of this Bill ; yes,
that may be true. But is that a reason why the Bill should not
be passed? Is there no such thing as the temptation to drunkenness ? If the condition of the people with regard to the use of
spirituous liquors has been improved to such a point that they
are, almost without exception, desirous to set aside the temptation, would it not be a cruel thing on the part of Parliament if we,
on the invitation of honourable members who do not represent
Wales, and have no title to speak on its behalf, were to refuse to
set that temptation aside ?

Mr. Gladstone has exactly hit the point. If the people
of Wales had not already made great progress in their
love of temperance they would never have demanded
the measure with such practical unanimity. From the
borough of Merthyr, referred to by the Reviewer—perhaps not without a purpose—petitions were sent in
favour of the Bill signed by 21,450, and in one part of
that borough, Aberdare, there was a general house-to-
house canvass with the following remarkable result.
Number of canvass papers filled in was 5,051. Of these
4,659 were in favour of Sunday-closing, 210 were against,
182 were neutral ; that is, 92 per cent. for closing, 4 per
cent. against, and about 4 per cent. neutral. When
these returns were classified they revealed the following
very striking result : that of 2,138 colliers who are
householders in Aberdare, no fewer than 1,976 approved
of Sunday-closing during the whole day, while 91 only
opposed, and 71 were neutral. Of artisan householders,
776 are for closing, 34 against, 23 neutral. Of labourers,
hauliers, &c., 659 are for, 28 against, and 24 neutral.
Of farmers, 33 are for, none against. Of railway servants, 176 are for, 10 against, 14 neutral. Even among
the publicans themselves we find 45 for, 28 against, and
12 neutral. Now we venture to submit that a popula
tion who could act in this way must, as Mr. Gladstone
says, have been already " improved " to a rather high
point as regards the use of spirituous liquors, and, we

dare to add, that they were so improved very largely
through the " influence and inner workings " of Dissent.
With regard to the general question, it is not very
easy to find definite statistics as to the social habits of a
people. But there are one or two facts that have
recently come to our knowledge which are not without
significance, as bearing on the sobriety of the Welsh
people. The Deputy Chief Constable for the county of
Glamorgan has lately stated that at the time of the
visit of the Prince of Wales to Swansea last year, he
was on duty from 6 a.m. until 2 a.m. the following
morning, and during the whole day and night he did not
see a single drunken man or woman ; and although it
was estimated that 100,000 people visited the town
during the day and night from the counties of Mòn-
mouth, Glamorgan, Brecknock, Carmarthen, Cardigan,
and Pembroke, there was no person apprehended
for drunkenness. Here is another fact. During the
National Eisteddfod meeting at Merthyr, in 1881, there
was an extraordinary influx of visitors from almost
every county in Wales. In course of the four days on
which the meetings were held, the Great Western, the
Midland, the London and North Western, and the Taff
Vale Railway Companies carried nearly 20,000 pas-
sengers in and out of the town, and on one of those
days, the day of the Choral Competition, upwards of
10,000 tickets were collected at the Merthyr railway
stations, yet during the whole week there were only
three persons apprehended by the police ; one of whom
was a tramp, and the two others Irish labourers who
had annoyed their employer. But none of these three
were apprehended for drunkenness.
    But we have a word more to say on the question of
Temperance. It must not be forgotten that the intemperance which this writer insinuates rather than asserts,

to abound in Wales is referred to as " a revelation of the
inner workings of Dissent." Now, perhaps in no part
of the world has the cause of Temperance been carried
on with so much energy, and, happily, we may add, with
so much success as it has been in Wales. But by
whom? We have before us an article which appeared
a little more than a twelvemonth ago in a Welsh
Quarterly, *Y Traethodydd*, from which the Reviewer is
fond of quoting. It is a history of the origin and progress of the Temperance movement in Wales. We cite
two or three sentences :—

> The most remarkable thing in connection with the Temperance
> cause in Wales, and it goes far to explain its extraordinary suc-
> cess, was the admirable readiness with which the ministers of the
> Gospel and the leading men in the different religious denomina-
> tions took it up and laboured for it. . . . The clergymen of
> the Church of England generally looked upon the thing with a
> good deal of contempt. I can remember only one Welsh clergy-
> man who took any interest in it, the Rev. Henry Griffith, of
> Landrygarn, a man greatly beloved, and "made perfect in every
> good work." Some Nonconformist ministers were unwilling to
> give up what they thought wholesome beverage. But as for those
> good and holy men who among the different sects had won most
> thoroughly the love and confidence of their countrymen, and who
> by their ability, zeal, and devotedness wielded such extraordinary
> power over them, they from the first threw themselves into the
> work, and nobly did they labour for it. Such men as John Elias,
> Henry Rees, and Ebenezer Richard* among the Calvinistic
> Methodists; Dr. Arthur Jones and William Williams of Wern
> among the Independents; Christmas Evans and Dr. Pritchard
> among the Baptists; and Lot Hughes and William Rowlands
> among the Wesleyans, at once recognised in this movement the
> guidance of providence and took to it as the work of God.

Another early and eminent champion of this good cause
says :—" In the *Dirwestydd*, a Temperance magazine,
for 1837 and 1838, there will be found the names of all
the ministers of all denominations in North Wales who
were pledged abstainers. They number about five hundred, and there is only one clergyman of the Church of

---

* Father of the member for Merthyr.

England in the whole list "—the Rev. Henry Griffith already mentioned. " For the first ten years in the history of the Temperance movement in North Wales, I don't think another clergyman could be found." So that, after all, it looks as if " the inner working of Dissent " had really been in favour of sobriety instead of the contrary, and that Dissent was left pretty much to struggle alone in this holy war, while " the authorised teachers of the people " stood aside jeering at the workers, or passing by on the other side in utter indifference.

There is one more matter which we must touch, though it is one difficult fully to discuss. Mr. Richard, in his lecture at the Memorial Hall, after referring to the remarkable absence of crime in Wales, said, " With regard to another point on which it is thought our country is most vulnerable, the question of morality as between the two sexes, I must denounce the grossly exaggerated representations that have been made on that point as groundless and calumnious. Things are not in that respect as the best friends of Wales desire and are diligently labouring to produce. But I assert, and have elsewhere proved, that with all our shortcomings Wales will compare advantageously with almost any part of England." This, like every other statement made in favour or in defence of the Principality, is flouted by the Reviewer. He had not failed to search for and exultingly display any strong sentences which had appeared in the form of deep lamentation, in Nonconformist publications, thirty years ago—or, as he says, from 1851 to 1856—that might seem to give countenance to the charge alluded to. But he knew, or might have known, that Mr. Richard's refutation had been before the public for sixteen years, and that it referred to nearly the very period specified by himself.

"We will not ask for his proofs," says the Reviewer. Well, they shall be given unasked. In his "Letters on the Social and Political Condition of the Principality of Wales," Mr. Richard has dealt with this subject at large, and in justice to our calumniated fellow-countrymen in Wales, we must allow him to speak for himself. The imputation, and the only imputation, was that illegitimacy was in astounding excess in Wales as compared with other parts of the kingdom.*

With all this, there are, no doubt, evils enough in Wales, as in every country under the sun, requiring to be remedied. There remains an amount of ignorance, irreligion, and immorality, to the removal of which the attention of the members of the Church of England may be directed with more profitable purpose than in vilifying the character and jeering at the labours of others who are working to the same end.

It is very obvious with what deadly effect the charges laid to the door of Nonconformity, as to the condition of the country, may be retorted on the Church. Very truly and pertinently we may say, "If the moral and religious character of the people be such as you insinuate, what account do you give of your own ministrations? For upwards of three centuries you, as the Protestant Church Establishment, have had the Principality of Wales under your spiritual care. For a large portion of that time you had the field almost wholly to yourselves, excepting the few scattered Nonconformists whom your predecessors hated and harried and hunted 'as one doth hunt a partridge over the mountains.'

---

* Here, in the original article as it appeared in *The British Quarterly Review,* there were inserted several extracts from the "Letters on the Social and Political Condition of Wales," which need not be repeated, as they will be found on pp. 61-70 of this volume.

During the whole of that time you had the patronage of the State, which you say is of such supreme importance to the conservation of religion and piety in the land ; you had all the ecclesiastical and educational endowments of the country in your hands; you had all the gradations of your hierarchy, including bishops and deans and archdeacons, &c., which you deem essential to the completeness and efficiency of a Christian Church; you had the higher and wealthier classes of the community, almost without exception, in your ranks ; you had a race of people under your charge who, as their whole history proves, are eager for instruction, and singularly accessible to religious impression and emotion ; you had the parochial system in operation which divided the country into convenient districts over which you claimed to exercise authority both by civil and ecclesiastical law.   And with all these advantages in your favour what have *you* to show ?   If the country be in the deplorable state which you not only confess, but loudly and almost vauntingly proclaim, what can you have to say, except to admit one of two things—either that your system is wholly unsuited to such a country as Wales, and such a people as the Welsh, or that you have failed utterly and ignominiously to work it to any good purpose."

The members of the Church of England in Wales have been, for some years past, making very strenuous, but hitherto very unsuccessful efforts, to allure the Welsh people from the folds of Dissent to their own. But certainly such articles as that in the *Church Quarterly* will hardly help them in the process.   What their Church has done is this.   First, for many generations, it utterly neglected the spiritual interests of those committed to its charge.   Then, when others had done the work it had failed to do, it strove to dispossess them of their labours. And finally, having miscarried in that aim, through the loyalty of the people to those who had "cared for their souls," they hold up the country to dishonour and contempt before the English people by unfair suppression of its virtues, and gross exaggeration of its shortcomings and defects. We can hardly imagine anything more like to hasten and to deepen the cry for disestablishment of the Church in Wales.

W. SPEAIGHT & SONS, PRINTERS, FETTER LANE, LONDON.

19